A YEAR OF CELEBRATION AND SPECTACLE

Ruskin Bond is known for his signature simplistic and witty writing style. He is the author of several bestselling short stories, novellas, collections, essays and children's books; and has contributed a number of poems and articles to various magazines and anthologies. At the age of 23, he won the prestigious John Llewellyn Rhys Prize for his first novel, *The Room on the Roof*. He was also the recipient of the Padma Shri in 1999, Lifetime Achievement Award by the Delhi Government in 2012 and the Padma Bhushan in 2014.

Born in 1934, Ruskin Bond grew up in Jamnagar, Shimla, New Delhi and Dehradun. Apart from three years in the UK, he has spent all his life in India and now lives in Landour, Mussoorie, with his adopted family.

RUSKIN
BOND
A YEAR OF CELEBRATION AND SPECTACLE

RUPA

Published by
Rupa Publications India Pvt. Ltd 2025
7/16, Ansari Road, Daryaganj
New Delhi 110002

Sales centres:
Bengaluru Chennai
Hyderabad Jaipur Kathmandu
Kolkata Mumbai Prayagraj

P-ISBN: 978-93-6156-113-9
E-ISBN: 978-93-6156-371-3

First impression 2025

10 9 8 7 6 5 4 3 2 1

The moral right of the author has been asserted.

CONTENTS

INTRODUCTION

As we teeter on the brink of a new year, several emotions surface—anticipation and nervousness, and also nostalgia. We can't help but reflect on all the ways in which time has changed us, or we have changed with time. At the same time, it is a moment of celebration and merrymaking, of coming together with our loved ones to commemorate endings, beginnings, and life itself, with all of the possibilities and joy sparkling in the air like the fireworks that go off at midnight.

Celebrating this spirit of reflection, *A Year of Celebration and Spectacle* brings together a selection of my most striking memories and fictional stories—from awe-inspiring tales to hilarious recollections, to reflections on the quieter moments of contentment—a collection as eclectic as all the moments that make up a year well lived. 'Calypso Christmas' and 'Party Time in Mussoorie' recall memories of some of my favourite get-togethers with my loved ones, while 'Bhabiji's House' and 'Bus Stop, Pipalnagar' are about celebrating the joys of everyday life with the people you care about. There are also stories like 'The Great Indian Rope Trick' and 'Nina', which explore the unique convergence of spectacle, entertainment and mystique that is only found in India. On the flip side are stories like 'When the Monsoon Breaks' and 'The Blue Umbrella', which contain ruminations on the glorious spectacle of nature itself, and the unforgettable quality of kindness and friendship.

As the years add up and the inexorable passage of time takes us along, it is easy to get caught up in anxieties about the future, and regrets about the past. But I hope you take a moment to pause, reflect, and celebrate how far you've come, and let the stories here kindle your memories, of times past and the people who have made you who you are.

Ruskin Bond

CALYPSO CHRISTMAS

My first Christmas in London had been a lonely one. My small bed-sitting-room near Swiss Cottage had been cold and austere, and my landlady had disapproved of any sort of revelry. Moreover, I hadn't the money for the theatre or a good restaurant. That first English Christmas was spent sitting in front of a lukewarm gas-fire, eating beans on toast, and drinking cheap sherry. My one consolation was the row of Christmas cards on the mantelpiece—most of them from friends in India.

But the following year I was making more money and living in a bigger, brighter, homelier room. The new landlady approved of my bringing friends—even girls—to the house, and had even made me a plum pudding so that I could entertain my guests. My friends in London included a number of Indian and Commonwealth students, and through them I met George, a friendly, sensitive person from Trinidad.

George was not a student. He was over thirty. Like thousands of other West Indians, he had come to England because he had been told that jobs were plentiful, that there was a free health scheme and national insurance, and that he could earn anything from ten to twenty pounds a week—far more than he could make in Trinidad or Jamaica. But, while it was true that jobs were to be had in England, it was also true that sections of local labour resented outsiders filling these posts. There were also those, belonging chiefly to the lower-middle classes, who were prone to various prejudices, and though these people were a minority, they were still capable of making themselves felt and heard.

In any case, London is a lonely place, especially for the stranger. And for the happy-go-lucky West Indian, accustomed to sunshine, colour and music, London must be quite baffling.

As though to match the grey-green fogs of winter, Londoners wore sombre colours, greys and browns. The West Indians couldn't understand this. Surely, they reasoned, during a grey season the colours worn should be vivid reds and greens—colours that would defy the curling fog and uncomfortable rain? But Londoners frowned on these gay splashes of colour; to them it all seemed an expression of some sort of barbarism. And then again Londoners had a horror of any sort of loud noise, and a blaring radio could (quite justifiably) bring in scores of protests from neighbouring houses. The West Indians, on the other hand, liked letting off steam; they liked holding parties in their rooms at which there was much singing and shouting. They had always believed that England was their mother country, and so, despite rain, fog, sleet and snow, they were determined to live as they had lived back home in Trinidad. And it is to their credit, and even to the credit of indigenous Londoners, that this is what they succeeded in doing.

George worked for British Railways. He was a ticket collector at one of the underground stations. He liked his work, and received about ten pounds a week for collecting tickets. A large, stout man, with huge hands and feet, he always had a gentle, kindly expression on his mobile face. Among other accomplishments, he could play the piano, and as there was an old, rather dilapidated piano in my room, he would often come over in the evenings to run his fat, heavy fingers over the keys, playing tunes that ranged from hymns to jazz pieces. I thought he would be a nice person to spend Christmas with, so I asked him to come and share the pudding my landlady had made, and a bottle of sherry I had procured.

Little did I realize that an invitation to George would be interpreted as an invitation to all of George's friends and relations—in fact, anyone who had known him in Trinidad—but this was the way he looked at it, and at eight o'clock on Christmas Eve, while a chilly wind blew dead leaves down from Hampstead Heath, I saw a veritable army of West Indians marching down Belsize Avenue, with George in the lead.

Bewildered, I opened my door to them; and in streamed George, George's cousins, George's nephews and George's friends. They were all smiling and they all shook hands with me, making complimentary remarks about my room ('Man, that's some piano!', 'Hey, look at that crazy picture!', 'This rocking chair gives me fever!') and took no time at all to feel and make themselves at home. Everyone had brought something along for the party. George had brought several bottles of beer. Eric, a flashy, coffee-coloured youth, had brought cigarettes and more beer. Marian, a buxom woman of thirty-five, who called me 'darling' as soon as we met, and kissed me on the cheeks saying she adored pink cheeks, had brought bacon and eggs. Her daughter Lucy, who was sixteen and in the full bloom of youth, had brought a gramophone, while the little nephews carried the records. Other friends and familiars had also brought beer; and one enterprising fellow produced a bottle of Jamaican rum.

Then everything began to happen at once.

Lucy put a record on the gramophone, and the strains of 'Basin Street Blues' filled the room. At the same time, George sat down at the piano to hammer out an accompaniment to the record. His huge hands crushed down on the keys as though he were chopping up hunks of meat. Marian had lit the gas-fire and was busy frying bacon and eggs. Eric was opening beer bottles. In the midst of the noise and confusion I heard a knock on the door—a very timid, hesitant sort of knock—and opening it, found my landlady standing on the threshold.

'Oh, Mr Bond, the neighbours—' she began, and glancing into the room was rendered speechless.

'It's only tonight,' I said. 'They'll all go home after an hour. Remember, it's Christmas!'

She nodded mutely and hurried away down the corridor, pursued by something called 'Be Bop A-Lula'. I closed the door and drew all the curtains in an effort to stifle the noise; but everyone was stamping about on the floorboards, and I hoped fervently that the downstairs people had gone to the theatre. George had started playing calypso music, and Eric and Lucy were strutting and stomping in the middle of the room, while the two nephews were improvising on their own. Before I knew what was happening, Marian had taken me in her strong arms and was teaching me to do the calypso. The song playing, I think, was 'Banana Boat Song'.

Instead of the party lasting an hour, it lasted three hours. We ate innumerable fried eggs and finished off all the beer. I took turns dancing with Marian, Lucy and the nephews. There was a peculiar expression they used when excited. 'Fire!' they shouted. I never knew what was supposed to be on fire, or what the exclamation implied, but I too shouted 'Fire!' and somehow it seemed a very sensible thing to shout.

Perhaps their hearts were on fire, I don't know; but for all their excitability and flashiness and brashness they were lovable and sincere friends, and today, when I look back on my two years in London, that Christmas party is the brightest, most vivid memory of all, and the faces of George and Marian, Lucy and Eric, are the faces I remember best.

At midnight someone turned out the light. I was dancing with Lucy at the time, and in the dark she threw her arms around me and kissed me full on the lips. It was the first time

I had been kissed by a girl, and when I think about it, I am glad that it was Lucy who kissed me.

When they left, they went in a bunch, just as they had come. I stood at the gate and watched them saunter down the dark, empty street. The buses and tubes had stopped running at midnight, and George and his friends would have to walk all the way back to their rooms at Highgate and Golders Green.

After they had gone, the street was suddenly empty and silent, and my own footsteps were the only sounds I could hear. The cold came clutching at me, and I turned up my collar. I looked up at the windows of my house, and at the windows of all the other houses in the street. They were all in darkness. It seemed to me that we were the only ones who had really celebrated Christmas.

WHO KISSED ME IN THE DARK?

This chapter, or story, could not have been written but for a phone call I received last week. I'll come to the caller later. Suffice to say that it triggered off memories of a hilarious fortnight in the autumn of that year (can't remember which one) when India and Pakistan went to war with each other. It did not last long, but there was plenty of excitement in our small town, set off by a rumour that enemy parachutists were landing in force in the ravine below Pari Tibba.

The road to this ravine led past my dwelling, and one afternoon I was amazed to see the town's constabulary, followed by hundreds of concerned citizens (armed mostly with hockey sticks) taking the trail down to the little stream where I usually went bird-watching. The parachutes turned out to be bedsheets from a nearby school, spread out to dry by the dhobis who lived on the opposite hill. After days of incessant rain the sun had come out, and the dhobis had finally got a chance to dry the school bedsheets on the verdant hillside. From afar they did look a bit like open parachutes. In times of crisis, it's wonderful what the imagination will do.

There were also black-outs. It's hard for a hill station to black itself out, but we did our best. Two or three respectable people were arrested for using their torches to find their way home in the dark. And of course, nothing could be done about the lights on the next mountain, as the people there did not even know there was a war on. They did not have radio or television or even electricity. They used kerosene lamps or lit bonfires!

We had a smart young set in Mussoorie in those days, mostly college students who had also been to convent schools, and some of them decided it would be a good idea to put on a show—or old-fashioned theatrical extravaganza—to raise funds for the war effort. And they thought it would be a good idea to rope me in, as I was the only writer living in Mussoorie in those innocent times. I was thirty-one and I had never been a college student but they felt I was the right person to direct a one-act play in English. This was to be the centrepiece of the show.

I forget the name of the play. It was one of those drawing-room situation comedies popular from the 1920s, inspired by such successes as *Charley's Aunt* and *Tons of Money*. Anyway, we went into morning rehearsals at Hakman's, one of the older hotels, where there was a proper stage and a hall large enough to seat at least two hundred spectators.

The participants were full of enthusiasm, and rehearsals went along quite smoothly. They were an engaging bunch of young people—Guttoo, the intellectual among them; Ravi, a schoolteacher; Gita, a tiny ball of fire; Neena, a heavy-footed Bharatnatyam exponent; Nellie, daughter of a nurse; Chameli, who was in charge of make-up (she worked in a local beauty salon); Rajiv, who served in the bar and was also our prompter; and a host of others, some of whom would sing and dance before and after our one-act play.

The performance was well attended, Ravi having rounded up a number of students from the local schools; and the lights were working, although we had to cover all doors, windows and exits with blankets to maintain the regulatory black-out. But the stage was old and rickety and things began to go wrong during Neena's dance number when, after a dazzling pirouette, she began stamping her feet and promptly went through the floorboards. Well, to be precise, her lower half went through, while the rest of her remained above board and visible to the audience.

The schoolboys cheered, the curtain came down and we rescued Neena, who had to be sent to the civil hospital with a sprained ankle, Mussoorie's only civilian war casualty.

There was a hold-up, but before the audience could get too restless the curtain went up on our play, a tea-party scene, which opened with Guttoo pouring tea for everyone. Unfortunately, our stage manager had forgotten to put any tea in the pot and poor Guttoo looked terribly put out as he went from cup to cup, pouring invisible tea. 'Damn. What happened to the tea?' muttered Guttoo, a line, which was not in the script. 'Never mind,' said Gita, playing opposite him and keeping her cool. 'I prefer my milk without tea,' and proceeded to pour herself a cup of milk.

After this, everyone began to fluff their lines and our prompter had a busy time. Unfortunately, he'd helped himself to a couple of rums at the bar, so that, whenever one of the actors faltered, he'd call out the correct words in a stentorian voice which could be heard all over the hall. Soon there was more prompting than acting and the audience began joining in with dialogue of their own.

Finally, to my great relief, the curtain came down—to thunderous applause. It went up again, and the cast stepped forward to take a bow. Our prompter, who was also the curtain-puller, released the ropes prematurely and the curtain came down with a rush, one of the sandbags hitting poor Guttoo on the head. He has never fully recovered from the blow.

The lights, which had been behaving all evening, now failed us, and we had a real black-out. In the midst of this confusion, someone—it must have been a girl, judging from the overpowering scent of jasmine that clung to her—put her arms around me and kissed me.

When the light came on again, she had vanished.

Who had kissed me in the dark?

As no one came forward to admit to the deed, I could only make wild guesses. But it had been a very sweet kiss, and I would have been only too happy to return it had I known its ownership. I could hardly go up to each of the girls and kiss them in the hope of reciprocation. After all, it might even have been someone from the audience.

Anyway, our concert did raise a few hundred rupees for the war effort. By the time we sent the money to the right authorities, the war was over. Hopefully they saw to it that the money was put to good use.

We went our various ways and although the kiss lingered in my mind, it gradually became a distant, fading memory and as the years passed it went out of my head altogether. Until the other day, almost forty years later...

'Phone for you,' announced Gautam, my seven-year-old secretary.

'Boy or girl? Man or woman?'

'Don't know. Deep voice like my teacher but it says you know her.'

'Ask her name.'

Gautam asked.

'She's Nellie, and she's speaking from Bareilly.'

'Nellie from Bareilly?' I was intrigued. I took the phone. 'Hello,' I said. 'I'm Bonda from Golconda.'

'Then you must be wealthy now.' Her voice was certainly husky. 'But don't you remember me? Nellie? I acted in that play of yours, up in Mussoorie a long time ago.'

'Of course, I remember now,' I was remembering. 'You had a small part, the maidservant I think. You were very pretty.

You had dark, sultry eyes. But what made you ring me after all these years?'

'Well, I was thinking of you. I've often thought about you. You were much older than me, but I liked you. After that show, when the lights went out, I came up to you and kissed you. And then I ran away.'

'So it was you! I've often wondered. But why did you run away? I would have returned the kiss. More than once.'

'I was very nervous. I thought you'd be angry.'

'Well, I suppose it's too late now. You must be happily married with lots of children.'

'Husband left me. Children grew up, went away.'

'It must be lonely for you.'

'I have lots of dogs.'

'How many?'

'About thirty.'

'Thirty dogs! Do you run a kennel club?'

'No, they are all strays. I run a dog shelter.'

'Well, that's very good of you. Very humane.'

'You must come and see it sometime. Come to Bareilly. Stay with me. You like dogs, don't you?'

'Er—yes, of course. Man's best friend, the dog. But thirty is a lot of dogs to have about the house.'

'I have lots of space.'

'I'm sure... well, Nellie, if ever I'm in Bareilly, I'll come to see you. And I'm glad you phoned and cleared up the mystery. It was a lovely kiss and I'll always remember it.'

We said our goodbyes and I promised to visit her some day. A trip to Bareilly to return a kiss might seem a bit far-fetched, but I've done sillier things in my life. It's those dogs that worry me. I can imagine them snapping at my heels as I attempt to approach their mistress. Dogs can be very possessive.

'Who was that on the phone?' asked Gautam, breaking in on my reverie.

'Just an old friend!'

'Dada's old girlfriend. Are you going to see her?'

'I'll think about it.'

And I'm still thinking about it and about those dogs. But bliss it was to be in Mussoorie forty years ago, when Nellie kissed me in the dark.

Some memories are best left untouched.

FROM SMALL BEGINNINGS

And the last puff of the day-wind brought from the
unseen villages, the scent of damp wood-smoke, hot cakes,
dripping undergrowth, and rotting pine cones. That is the
true smell of the Himalayas, and if once it creeps into
the blood of a man, that man will at the last, forgetting
all else, return to the hills to die.

—Rudyard Kipling

On the first clear September day, towards the end of the
rains, I visited the pine knoll, my place of peace and power.
It was months since I'd last been there. Trips to the plains,
a crisis in my affairs, involvements with other people and their
troubles, and an entire monsoon had come between me and the
grassy, pine-topped slope facing the Hill of Fairies (Pari Tibba
to the locals). Now I tramped through late monsoon foliage—
tall ferns, bushes festooned with flowering convolvulus—crossed
the stream by way of its little bridge of stones and climbed the
steep hill to the pine slope.

When the trees saw me, they made as if to turn in my
direction. A puff of wind came across the valley from the distant
snows. A long-tailed blue magpie took alarm and flew noisily out
of an oak tree. The cicadas were suddenly silent. But the trees
remembered me. They bowed gently in the breeze and beckoned
me nearer, welcoming me home. Three pines, a straggling oak
and a wild cherry. I went among them and acknowledged their
welcome with a touch of my hand against their trunks—the

cherry's smooth and polished; the pine's patterned and whorled; the oak's rough, gnarled, full of experience. He'd been there longest, and the wind had bent his upper branches and twisted a few, so that he looked shaggy and undistinguished. But like the philosopher who is careless about his dress and appearance, the oak has secrets, a hidden wisdom. He has learnt the art of survival!

While the oak and the pines are older than me and have been here many years, the cherry tree is exactly seven years old. I know because I planted it.

One day I had this cherry seed in my hand, and on an impulse I thrust it into the soft earth, and then went away and forgot all about it. A few months later I found a tiny cherry tree in the long grass. I did not expect it to survive. But the following year it was two feet tall. And then some goats ate its leaves, and a grass cutter's scythe injured the stem, and I was sure it would wither away. But it renewed itself, sprang up even faster, and within three years it was a healthy, growing tree, about five feet tall.

I left the hills for two years—forced by circumstances to make a living in Delhi—but this time I did not forget the cherry tree. I thought about it fairly often, sent telepathic messages of encouragement in its direction. And when, a couple of years ago, I returned in the autumn, my heart did a somersault when I found my tree sprinkled with pale pink blossom. (The Himalayan cherry flowers in November.) And later, when the fruit was ripe, the tree was visited by finches, tits, bulbuls and other small birds, all come to feast on the sour, red cherries.

Last summer I spent a night on the pine knoll, sleeping on the grass beneath the cherry tree. I lay awake for hours, listening to the chatter of the stream and the occasional tonk-tonk of a nightjar, and watching, through the branches overhead, the stars turning in the sky; I felt the power of the sky and earth, and the power of a small cherry seed...

And so when the rains are over, this is where I come, that I might feel the peace and power of this place. It's a big world and momentous events are taking place all the time. But this is where I have seen it happen.

This is where I will write my stories. I can see everything from here—my cottage across the valley; behind and above me, the town and the bazaar straddling the ridge; to the left, the high mountains and the twisting road to the source of the great river; below me, the little stream and the path to the village; ahead, the Hill of Fairies, the fields beyond; the wide valley below, and then another range of hills and then the distant plains. I can even see Prem Singh in the garden, putting the mattresses out in the sun.

From here he is just a speck on the far hill, but I know it is Prem by the way he stands. A man may have a hundred disguises, but in the end it is his posture that gives him away. Like my grandfather, who was a master of disguise and successfully roamed the bazaars as fruit vendor or basket maker; but we could always recognize him because of his pronounced slouch.

Prem Singh doesn't slouch, but he has this habit of looking up at the sky (regardless of whether it's cloudy or clear), and at the moment he's looking at the sky.

Eight years with Prem! He was just a sixteen-year-old boy when I first saw him, and now he has a wife and child.

I had been in the cottage for just over a year... He stood on the landing outside the kitchen door. A tall boy, dark, with good teeth and brown, deep-set eyes; dressed smartly in white drill—his only change of clothes. Looking for a job. I liked the look of him, but—

'I already have someone working for me,' I said.

'Yes, sir. He is my uncle.'

In the hills, everyone is a brother or an uncle.

'You don't want me to dismiss your uncle?'

'No, sir. But he says you can find a job for me.'

'I'll try. I'll make inquiries. Have you just come from your village?'

'Yes. Yesterday I walked ten miles to Pauri. There I got a bus.'

'Sit down. Your uncle will make some tea.'

He sat down on the steps, removed his white keds, wriggled his toes. His feet were both long and broad, large feet, but not ugly. He was unusually clean for a hill boy. And taller than most.

'Do you smoke?' I asked.

'No, sir.'

'It is true,' said his uncle, 'he does not smoke. All my nephews smoke, but this one, he is a little peculiar, he does not smoke—neither beedi nor hookah.'

'Do you drink?'

'It makes me vomit.'

'Do you take bhang?'

'No, sahib.'

'You have no vices. It's unnatural.'

'He is unnatural, sahib,' said his uncle.

'Does he chase girls?'

'They chase him, sahib.'

'So he left the village and came looking for a job.' I looked at him. He grinned, then looked away, began rubbing his feet.

'Your name is?'

'Prem Singh.'

'All right, Prem, I will try to do something for you.'

I did not see him for a couple of weeks. I forgot about finding him a job. But when I met him again, on the road to the bazaar, he told me that he had got a temporary job in the Survey, looking after the surveyor's tents.

'Next week we will be going to Rajasthan,' he said.

'It will be very hot. Have you been in the desert before?'

'No, sir.'

'It is not like the hills. And it is far from home.'

'I know. But I have no choice in the matter. I have to collect some money in order to get married.'

In his region there was a bride price, usually of two thousand rupees.

'Do you have to get married so soon?'

'I have only one brother and he is still very young. My mother is not well. She needs a daughter-in-law to help her in the fields and with the cows and in the house. We are a small family, so the work is greater.'

Every family has its few terraced fields, narrow and stony, usually perched on a hillside above a stream or river. They grow rice, barley, maize, potatoes—just enough to live on. Even if their produce is sufficient for marketing, the absence of roads makes it difficult to get the produce to the market towns. There is no money to be earned in the villages, and money is needed for clothes, soap, medicines, and for recovering the family jewellery from the moneylenders. So the young men leave their villages to find work, and to find work they must go to the plains. The lucky ones get into the army. Others enter domestic service or take jobs in garages, hotels, wayside tea shops, schools...

In Mussoorie the main attraction is the large number of schools, which employ cooks and bearers. But the schools were full when Prem arrived. He'd been to the recruiting centre at Roorkee, hoping to get into the army; but they found a deformity in his right foot, the result of a bone broken when a landslip carried him away one dark monsoon night; he was lucky, he said, that it was only his foot and not his head that had been broken.

He came to the house to inform his uncle about the job and

to say goodbye. I thought: another nice person I probably won't see again; another ship passing in the night, the friendly twinkle of its lights soon vanishing in the darkness. I said 'come again', held his smile with mine so that I could remember him better, and returned to my study and my typewriter. The typewriter is the repository of a writer's loneliness. It stares unsympathetically back at him every day, doing its best to be discouraging. Maybe I'll go back to the old-fashioned quill pen and marble inkstand; then I can feel like a real writer, Balzac or Dickens, scratching away into the endless reaches of the night... Of course, the days and nights are seemingly shorter than they need to be! They must be, otherwise why do we hurry so much and achieve so little, by the standards of the past...

Prem goes, disappears into the vast faceless cities of the plains, and a year slips by, or rather I do, and then here he is again, thinner and darker and still smiling and still looking for a job. I should have known that hill men don't disappear altogether. The spirit-haunted rocks don't let their people wander too far, lest they lose them forever.

I was able to get him a job in the school. The Headmaster's wife needed a cook. I wasn't sure if Prem could cook very well but I sent him along and they said they'd give him a trial. Three days later the Headmaster's wife met me on the road and started gushing all over me. She was the type who gushes.

'We're so grateful to you! Thank you for sending me that lovely boy. He's so polite. And he cooks very well. A little too hot for my husband, but otherwise delicious—just delicious! He's a real treasure—a lovely boy.' And she gave me an arch look—the famous look that she used to captivate all the good-looking young prefects who became prefects, it was said, only if she approved of them.

I wasn't sure that she didn't want something more than a

cook, and I only hoped that Prem would give every satisfaction.

He looked cheerful enough when he came to see me on his off-day.

'How are you getting on?' I asked.

'Lovely,' he said, using his mistress's favourite expression.

'What do you mean—lovely? Do they like your work?'

'The memsahib likes it. She strokes me on the cheek whenever she enters the kitchen. The sahib says nothing. He takes medicine after every meal.'

'Did he always take medicine—or only now that you're doing the cooking?'

'I am not sure. I think he has always been sick.'

He was sleeping in the Headmaster's verandah and getting sixty rupees a month. A cook in Delhi got a hundred and sixty. And a cook in Paris or New York got ten times as much. I did not say as much to Prem. He might ask me to get him a job in New York. And that would be the last I saw of him! He, as a cook, might well get a job making curries off Broadway; I, as a writer, wouldn't get to first base. And only my Uncle Ken knew the secret of how to make a living without actually doing any work. But then, of course, he had four sisters. And each of them was married to a fairly prosperous husband. So Uncle Ken divided his year among them. Three months with Aunt Ruby in Nainital. Three months with Aunt Susie in Kashmir. Three months with my mother (not quite so affluent) in Jamnagar. And three months in the Vet Hospital in Bareilly, where Aunt Mabel ran the hospital for her veterinary husband. In this way, he never overstayed his welcome. A sister can look after a brother for just three months at a time and no more. Uncle Ken had it worked out to perfection.

But I had no sisters and I couldn't live forever on the royalties of a single novel. So I had to write others. So I came to the hills.

The hill men go to the plains to make a living. I had to come to the hills to try and make mine.

'Prem,' I said, 'why don't you work for me?'

'And what about my uncle?'

'He seems ready to desert me any day. His grandfather is ill, he says, and he wants to go home.'

'His grandfather died last year.'

'That's what I mean—he's getting restless. And I don't mind if he goes. These days he seems to be suffering from a form of sleeping sickness. I have to get up first and make his tea...'

Sitting here under the cherry tree, whose leaves are just beginning to turn yellow, I rest my chin on my knees and gaze across the valley to where Prem moves about in the garden. Looking back over the seven years he has been with me, I recall some of the nicest things about him. They come to me in no particular order—just pieces of cinema—coloured slides slipping across the screen of memory...

Prem rocking his infant son to sleep—crooning to him, passing his large hand gently over the child's curly head—Prem following me down to the police station when I was arrested (on a warrant from Bombay, charging me with writing an allegedly obscene short story!), and waiting outside until I reappeared; his smile, when I found him in Delhi, his large, irrepressible laughter, most in evidence when he was seeing an old Laurel and Hardy movie.

Of course, there were times when he could be infuriating, stubborn, deliberately pig-headed, sending me little notes of resignation—but I never found it difficult to overlook these little acts of self-indulgence. He had brought much love and laughter into my life, and what more could a lonely man ask for?

It was his stubborn streak that limited the length of his stay in the Headmaster's household. Mr Good was tolerant enough. But Mrs Good was one of those women who, when they are pleased with you, go out of their way to help, pamper and flatter; and who, when they are displeased, become vindictive, going out of their way to harm or destroy. Mrs Good sought power—over her husband, her dog, her favourite pupils, her servant... She had absolute power over the husband and the dog, partial power over her slightly bewildered pupils; and none at all over Prem, who missed the subtleties of her designs upon his soul. He did not respond to her mothering, or to the way in which she tweaked him on the cheeks, brushed against him in the kitchen and made admiring remarks about his looks and physique. Memsahibs, he knew, were not for him. So he kept a stony face and went diligently about his duties. And she felt slighted, put in her place. Her liking turned to dislike. Instead of admiring remarks, she began making disparaging remarks about his looks, his clothes, his manners. She found fault with his cooking. No longer was it 'lovely'. She even accused him of taking away the dog's meat and giving it to a poor family living on the hillside—no more heinous crime could be imagined! Mr Good threatened him with dismissal. So Prem became stubborn. The following day he withheld the dog's food altogether; threw it down the *khud* where it was seized upon by innumerable strays, and went off to the pictures.

It was the end of his job. 'I'll have to go home now,' he told me. 'I won't get another job in this area. The *mem* will see to that.'

'Stay a few days,' I said.

'I have only enough money with which to get home.'

'Keep it for going home. You can stay with me for a few days, while you look around. Your uncle won't mind sharing his food with you.'

His uncle did mind. He did not like the idea of working for his nephew as well; it seemed to him no part of his duties. And he was apprehensive that Prem might get his job.

So Prem stayed no longer than a week.

Here on the knoll the grass is just beginning to turn October yellow. The first clouds approaching winter cover the sky. The trees are very still. The birds are silent. Only a cricket keeps singing on the oak tree. Perhaps there will be a storm before evening. A storm like that in which Prem arrived at the cottage with his wife and child—but that's jumping too far ahead...

After he had returned to his village, it was several months before I saw him again. His uncle told me he had taken a job in Delhi. There was an address. It did not seem complete, but I resolved that when I was next in Delhi I would try to see him.

The opportunity came in May, as the hot winds of summer blew across the plains. It was the time of year when people who can afford it, try to get away to the hills. I dislike New Delhi at the best of times, and I hate it in summer. People compete with each other in being bad-tempered and mean. But I had to go down—I don't remember why, but it must have seemed very necessary at the time—and I took the opportunity to try and see Prem.

Nothing went right for me. Of course the address was all wrong, and I wandered about in a remote, dusty, treeless colony called Vasant Vihar (Spring Garden) for over two hours, asking all the domestic servants I came across if they could put me in touch with Prem Singh of Village Koli, Pauri Garhwal. There were innumerable Prem Singhs, but apparently none who belonged to Village Koli. I returned to my hotel and took two days to recover from heatstroke before returning to Mussoorie, thanking God for mountains!

And then the uncle gave me notice. He'd found a better paid job in Dehra Dun and was anxious to be off. I didn't try to stop him.

For the next six months I lived in the cottage without any help. I did not find this difficult. I was used to living alone. It wasn't service that I needed but companionship. In the cottage it was very quiet. The ghosts of long-dead residents were sympathetic but unobtrusive. The song of the whistling thrush was beautiful, but I knew he was not singing for me. Up the valley came the sound of a flute, but I never saw the flute player. My affinity was with the little red fox who roamed the hillside below the cottage. I met him one night and wrote these lines:

As I walked home last night
I saw a lone fox dancing
In the cold moonlight.
I stood and watched—then
Took the low road, knowing
The night was his by right.
Sometimes, when words ring true,
I'm like a lone fox dancing
In the morning dew.

During the rains, watching the dripping trees and the mist climbing the valley, I wrote a great deal of poetry. Loneliness is of value to poets. But poetry didn't bring me much money, and funds were low. And then, just as I was wondering if I would have to give up my freedom and take a job again, a publisher bought the paperback rights of one of my children's stories, and I was free to live and write as I pleased—for another three months!

That was in November. To celebrate, I took a long walk through the Landour Bazaar and up the Tehri road. It was a good day for walking; and it was dark by the time I returned to the outskirts of the town. Someone stood waiting for me on the road above the cottage. I hurried past him.

If I am not for myself,
Who will be for me?
And if I am not for others,

What am I?
And if not now, when?

I startled myself with the memory of these words of Hillel, the ancient Hebrew sage. I walked back to the shadows where the youth stood, and saw that it was Prem.

'Prem!' I said. 'Why are you sitting out here, in the cold? Why did you not go to the house?'

'I went, sir, but there was a lock on the door. I thought you had gone away.'

'And you were going to remain here, on the road?'

'Only for tonight. I would have gone down to Dehra in the morning.'

'Come, let's go home. I have been waiting for you. I looked for you in Delhi, but could not find the place where you were working.'

'I have left them now.'

'And your uncle has left me. So will you work for me now?'

'For as long as you wish.'

'For as long as the gods wish.'

We did not go straight home, but returned to the bazaar and took our meal in the Sindhi Sweet Shop; hot *puris* and strong sweet tea.

We walked home together in the bright moonlight. I felt sorry for the little fox dancing alone.

That was twenty years ago, and Prem and his wife and three children are still with me. But we live in a different house now, on another hill.

BHABIJI'S HOUSE

My neighbours in Rajouri Garden back in the 1960s were the Kamal family. This entry from my journal, which I wrote on one of my later visits, describes a typical day in that household.

At first light there is a tremendous burst of birdsong from the guava tree in the little garden. Over a hundred sparrows wake up all at once and give tongue to whatever it is that sparrows have to say to each other at five o'clock on a foggy winter's morning in Delhi.

In the small house, people sleep on; that is, everyone except 'Bhabiji'—Granny—the head of the lively Punjabi middle-class family with whom I nearly always stay when I am in Delhi.

She coughs, stirs, groans, grumbles and gets out of bed. The fire has to be lit, and food prepared for two of her sons to take to work. There is her daughter-in-law, Shobha, to help her; but the girl is not very bright at getting up in the morning. Actually, it is this way: Bhabiji wants to show up her daughter-in-law; so, no matter how hard Shobha tries to be up first, Bhabiji forestalls her. The old lady does not sleep well, anyway; her eyes are open long before the first sparrow chirps, and as soon as she sees her daughter-in-law stirring, she scrambles out of bed and hurries to the kitchen. This gives her the opportunity to say: 'What good is a daughter-in-law when I have to get up to prepare her husband's food?'

The truth is that Bhabiji does not like anyone else preparing her sons' food. She looks no older than when I first saw her ten years ago. She still has complete control over a large family and, with tremendous confidence and enthusiasm, presides over the lives of three sons, a daughter, two daughters-in-law and fourteen grandchildren. This is a joint family (there are not many left in a big city like Delhi), in which the sons and their families all live together as one unit under their mother's benevolent (and sometimes slightly malevolent) autocracy. Even when her husband was alive, Bhabiji dominated the household.

The eldest son, Shiv, has a separate kitchen, but his wife and children participate in all the family celebrations and quarrels. It is a small miracle how everyone (including myself when I visit) manages to fit into the house; and a stranger might be forgiven for wondering where everyone sleeps, for no beds are visible during the day. That is because the beds—light wooden frames with rough string across—are brought in only at night, and are taken out first thing in the morning and kept in the garden shed.

As Bhabiji lights the kitchen fire, the household begins to stir, and Shobha joins her mother-in-law in the kitchen. As a guest I am privileged and may get up last. But my bed soon becomes an island battered by waves of scurrying, shouting children, eager to bathe, dress, eat and find their school books. Before I can get up, someone brings me a tumbler of hot sweet tea. It is a brass tumbler and burns my fingers; I have yet to learn how to hold one properly. Punjabis like their tea with lots of milk and sugar—so much so that I often wonder why they bother to add any tea.

Ten years ago, 'bed tea' was unheard of in Bhabiji's house. Then, the first time I came to stay, Kamal, the youngest son, told Bhabiji: 'My friend is Angrez. He must have tea in bed.' He forgot to mention that I usually took my morning cup at seven; they gave it to me at five. I gulped it down and went to sleep again. Then, slowly, others in the household began indulging in morning cups of tea. Now everyone, including the older children, has 'bed tea'. They bless my English forebears for instituting the custom; I bless the Punjabis for perpetuating it.

Breakfast is by rota, in the kitchen. It is a tiny room and accommodates only four adults at a time. The children have eaten first; but the smallest children, Shobha's toddlers, keep coming in and climbing over us. Says Bhabiji of the youngest and most mischievous: 'He lives only because God keeps a special eye on him.'

Kamal, his elder brother Arun, and I sit cross-legged and barefooted on the floor while Bhabiji serves us hot parathas stuffed with potatoes and onions, along with omelettes, an excellent dish. Arun then goes to work on his scooter, while Kamal catches a bus for the city, where he attends an art college. After they have gone, Bhabiji and Shobha have their breakfast.

By nine o'clock everyone who is still in the house is busy doing something. Shobha is washing clothes. Bhabiji has settled down on a cot with a huge pile of spinach, which she methodically cleans and chops up. Madhu, her fourteen-year-old granddaughter, who attends school only in the afternoons, is washing down the sitting room floor. Madhu's mother is a teacher in a primary school in Delhi, and earns a pittance of Rs 150 a month. Her husband went to England ten years ago, and never returned; he does not send any money home.

Madhu is made attractive by the gravity of her countenance. She is always thoughtful, reflective; seldom speaks, smiles rarely (but looks very pretty when she does). I wonder what she thinks about as she scrubs floors, prepares meals with Bhabiji, washes dishes and even finds a few hard-pressed moments for her schoolwork. She is the Cinderella of the house. Not that she has to put up with anything like a cruel stepmother. Madhu is Bhabiji's favourite. She has made herself so useful that she is above all reproach. Apart from that, there is a certain measure of aloofness about her—she does not get involved in domestic squabbles—and this is foreign to a household in which everyone has something to say for himself or herself. Her two young brothers are constantly being reprimanded; but no one says anything to Madhu. Only yesterday morning, when clothes were being washed and Madhu was scrubbing the floor, the following dialogue took place.

Madhu's mother (picking up a school book left in the courtyard): 'Where's that boy Popat? See how careless he is with his books! Popat! He's run off. Just wait till he gets back. I'll give him a good beating.'

Vinod's mother: 'It's not Popat's book. It's Vinod's. Where's Vinod?'

Vinod (grumpily): 'It's Madhu's book.'

Silence for a minute or two. Madhu continues scrubbing the floor; she does not bother to look up. Vinod picks up the book and takes it indoors. The women return to their chores.

Manju, daughter of Shiv and sister of Vinod, is averse to housework and, as a result, is always being scolded—by her parents, grandmother, uncles and aunts.

Now, she is engaged in the unwelcomed chore of sweeping the front yard. She does this with a sulky look, ignoring my cheerful remarks. I have been sitting under the guava tree, but Manju soon sweeps me away from this spot. She creates a drifting cloud of dust, and seems satisfied only when the dust settles on the clothes that have just been hung up to dry. Manju is a sensuous creature and like most sensuous people, is lazy by nature. She does not like sweeping because the boy next door can see her at it, and she wants to appear before him in a more glamorous light. Her first action every morning is to turn to the cinema advertisements in the newspaper. Bombay's movie moguls cater for girls like Manju who long to be tragic heroines. Life is so very dull for middle-class teenagers in Delhi that it is only natural that they should lean so heavily on escapist entertainment. Every residential area has a cinema. But there is not a single bookshop in this particular suburb, although it has a population of over twenty thousand literate people. Few children read books; but they are adept at swotting up examination 'guides'; and students of, say, Hardy or Dickens read the guides and not the novels.

Bhabiji is now grinding onions and chillies in a mortar. Her eyes are watering but she is in a good mood. Shobha sits quietly in the kitchen. A little while ago she was complaining to me of a backache. I am the only one who lends a sympathetic ear to complaints of aches and pains. But since last night, my sympathies have been under severe strain. When I got into bed at about ten o'clock, I found the sheets wet. Apparently Shobha had put her baby to sleep in my bed during the afternoon.

While the housework is still in progress, cousin Kishore arrives. He is an itinerant musician who makes a living by arranging performances at weddings. He visits Bhabiji's house frequently and at odd hours, often a little tipsy, always brimming over with goodwill and grandiose plans for the future. It was once his ambition to be a film producer, and some years back he lost a lot of Bhabiji's money in producing a film that was never completed. He still talks of finishing it.

'Brother,' he says, taking me into his confidence for the hundredth time, 'do you know anyone who has a movie camera?'

'No,' I say, knowing only too well how these admissions can lead me into a morass of complicated manoeuvres. But Kishore is not easily put off, especially when he has been fortified with country liquor.

'But you *knew* someone with a movie camera?' he asks.

'That was long ago.'

'How long ago?' (I have got him going now.)

'About five years back.'

'Only five years? Find him, find him!'

'It's no use. He doesn't have the movie camera any more. He sold it.'

'Sold it!' Kishore looks at me as though I have done him an injury. 'But why didn't you buy it? All we need is a movie camera, and our fortune is made. I will produce the film, I will direct it, I will write the music. Two in one, Charlie Chaplin and Raj Kapoor. Why didn't you buy the camera?'

'Because I didn't have the money.'

'But we could have borrowed the money.'

'If you are in a position to borrow money, you can go out and buy another movie camera.'

'We could have borrowed the camera. Do you know anyone else who has one?'

'Not a soul.' I am firm this time; I will not be led into another maze.

'Very sad, very sad,' mutters Kishore. And with a dejected, hangdog expression designed to make me feel that I am responsible for all his failures, he moves off.

Bhabiji had expressed some annoyance at his arrival, but he softens her up by leaving behind an invitation to a wedding party this evening. No one in the house knows the bride's or bridegroom's family, but that does not matter; knowing one of the musicians is just as good. Almost everyone will go.

While Bhabiji, Shobha and Madhu are preparing lunch, Bhabiji engages in one of her favourite subjects of conversation, Kamal's marriage, which she hopes she will be able to arrange in the near future. She freely acknowledges that she made grave blunders in selecting wives for her other sons—this is meant to be heard by Shobha—and promises not to repeat her mistakes. According to Bhabiji, Kamal's bride should be both educated and domesticated; and of course she must be fair.

'What if he likes a dark girl?' I ask teasingly.

Bhabiji looks horrified. 'He cannot marry a dark girl,' she declares.

'But dark girls are beautiful,' I tell her.

'Impossible!'

'Do you want him to marry a European girl?'

'No foreigners! I know them, they'll take my son away. He shall have a good Punjabi girl, with a complexion the colour of wheat.'

Noon. The shadows shift and cross the road. I sit beneath the guava tree and watch the women at work. They will not let me do anything, but they like talking to me and they love to hear my broken Punjabi. Sparrows flit about at their feet, snapping up the grain that runs away from their busy fingers. A crow looks speculatively at the empty kitchen, sidles towards the open door; but Bhabiji has only to glance up and the experienced crow flies away. He knows he will not be able to make off with anything from this house.

One by one the children come home, demanding food. Now it is Madhu's turn to go to school. Her younger brother Popat, an intelligent but undersized boy of thirteen, appears in the doorway and asks for lunch.

'Be off!' says Bhabiji. 'It isn't ready yet.'

Actually the food is ready and only the chapatis remain to be made. Shobha will attend to them. Bhabiji lies down on her cot in the sun, complaining of a pain in her back and ringing noises in her ears.

'I'll press your back,' says Popat. He has been out of Bhabiji's favour lately, and is looking for an opportunity to be rehabilitated.

Barefooted, he stands on Bhabiji's back and treads her weary flesh and bones with a gentle walking-in-one-spot movement. Bhabiji grunts with relief. Every day she has new pains in new places. Her age, and the daily business of feeding the family and running everyone's affairs, are beginning to tell on her. But she would sooner die than give up her position of dominance in the house. Her working sons still hand over their pay to her, and she dispenses the money as she sees fit.

The pummelling she gets from Popat puts her in a better mood, and she holds forth on another favourite subject, the respective merits of various dowries. Shiv's wife (according to Bhabiji) brought nothing with her but a string cot; Kishore's wife brought only a sharp and clever tongue; Shobha brought a wonderful steel cupboard, fully expecting that it would do all the housework for her.

This last observation upsets Shobha, and a little later I find her under the guava tree, weeping profusely. I give her the comforting words she obviously expects; but it is her husband Arun who will have to bear the brunt of her outraged feelings when he comes home this evening. He is rather nervous of his wife. Last night he wanted to eat out, at a restaurant, but did not want to be accused of wasting money; so he stuffed fifteen rupees into my pocket and asked me to invite both him and Shobha to dinner, which I did.

We had a good dinner. Such unexpected hospitality on my part has further improved my standing with Shobha. Now, in spite of other chores, she sees that I get cups of tea and coffee at odd hours of the day.

Bhabiji knows Arun is soft with his wife, and taunts him about it. She was saying this morning that whenever there is any work to be done Shobha retires to bed with a headache (partly true). She says even Manju does more housework (not true). Bhabiji has certain talents as an actress, and does a good take-off of Shobha sulking and grumbling at having too much to do.

While Bhabiji talks, Popat sneaks off and goes for a ride on the bicycle. It is a very old bicycle and is constantly undergoing repairs. 'The soul has gone out of it,' says Vinod philosophically and makes his way on to the roof, where he keeps a store of pornographic literature. Up there, he cannot be seen and cannot be remembered, and so avoids being sent out on errands.

One of the boys is bathing at the handpump. Manju, who should have gone to school with Madhu, is stretched out on a cot, complaining of fever. But she will be up in time to attend the wedding party...

Towards evening, as the birds return to roost in the guava tree, their chatter is challenged by the tumult of people in the house getting ready for the wedding party.

Manju presses her tight pyjamas but neglects to darn them. She wears a loose-fitting, diaphanous shirt. She keeps flitting in and out of the front room so that I can admire the way she glitters. Shobha has used too much powder and lipstick in an effort to look like the femme fatale that she indubitably is not. Shiv's more conservative wife floats around in loose, old-fashioned pyjamas. Bhabiji is sober and austere in a white sari. Madhu looks neat. The men wear their suits.

Popat is holding up a mirror for his Uncle Kishore, who is combing his long hair. (Kishore kept his hair long, like a court musician at the time of Akbar, before the hippies had been heard of.) He is nodding benevolently, having fortified himself from a bottle labelled 'Som Ras' ('Nectar of the Gods'), obtained cheaply from an illicit still.

Kishore: 'Don't shake the mirror, boy!'

Popat: 'Uncle, it's your head that's shaking.'

Shobha is happy. She loves going out, especially to weddings, and she always takes her two small boys with her, although they invariably spoil the carpets.

Only Kamal, Popat and I remain behind. I have had more than my share of wedding parties.

The house is strangely quiet. It does not seem so small now, with only three people left in it. The kitchen has been locked (Bhabiji will not leave it open while Popat is still in the house), so we visit the dhaba, the wayside restaurant near the main road, and this time I pay the bill with my own money. We have kababs and chicken curry.

Yesterday, Kamal and I took our lunch on the grass of the Buddha Jayanti Gardens (Buddha's Birthday Gardens). There was no college for Kamal, as the majority of Delhi's students had hijacked a number of corporation buses and headed for the Pakistan High Commission, with every intention of levelling it to the ground if possible, as a protest against the hijacking of an Indian plane from Srinagar to Lahore. The students were met by the Delhi police in full strength, and a pitched battle took place, in which stones from the students and tear gas shells from the police were the favoured missiles. There were two shells fired every minute, according to a newspaper report. And this went on all day. A number of students and policemen were injured, but by some miracle no one was killed. The police held their ground, and the Pakistan High Commission remained inviolate. But the Australian High Commission, situated to the rear of the student brigade, received most of the tear gas shells, and had to close down for the day.

Kamal and I attended the siege for about an hour, before retiring to the Gardens with our ham sandwiches. A couple of friendly squirrels came up to investigate and were soon taking bread from our hands. We could hear the chanting of the students in the distance. I lay back on the grass and opened my copy of *Barchester Towers*. Whenever life in Delhi, or in Bhabiji's house (or anywhere, for that matter), becomes too tumultuous, I turn to Trollope. Nothing could be further removed from the turmoil of our times than an English cathedral town in the nineteenth century. But I think Jane Austen would have appreciated life in Bhabiji's house.

By ten o'clock, everyone is back from the wedding. (They had gone for the feast, and not for the ceremonies, which continue into the early hours of the morning.) Shobha is full of praise for the bridegroom's good looks and fair complexion. She describes him as being *gora-chitta*—very white! She does not have a high opinion of the bride.

Shiv, in a happy and reflective mood, extols the qualities of his own wife, referring to her as the Barrel. He tells us how, shortly after their marriage, she had threatened to throw a brick at the next-door girl. This little incident remains fresh in Shiv's mind, after eighteen years of marriage.

He says: 'When the neighbours came and complained, I told them, "It is quite possible that my wife will throw a brick at your daughter. She is in the habit of throwing bricks." The neighbours held their peace.'

I think Shiv is rather proud of his wife's militancy when it comes to taking on neighbours; recently she vanquished the woman next door (a formidable Sikh lady) after a verbal battle that lasted three hours. But in arguments or quarrels with Bhabiji, Shiv's wife always loses, because Shiv takes his mother's side. Arun, on the other hand, is afraid of both wife and mother, and simply makes himself scarce when a quarrel develops. Or he tells his mother she is right, and then, to placate Shobha, takes her to the pictures.

Kishore turns up just as everyone is about to go to bed. Bhabiji is annoyed at first, because he has been drinking too much; but when he produces a bunch of cinema tickets, she is mollified and asks him to stay the night. Not even Bhabiji likes missing a new picture.

Kishore is urging me to write his life story.

'Your life would make a most interesting story,' I tell him. 'But it will be interesting only if I put in everything—your successes *and* your failures.'

'No, no, only successes,' exhorts Kishore. 'I want you to describe me as a popular music director.'

'But you have yet to become popular.'

'I will be popular if you write about me.'

Fortunately we are interrupted by the cots being brought in. Then Bhabiji and Shiv go into a huddle, discussing plans for building an extra room. After all, Kamal may be married soon.

One by one, the children get under their quilts. Popat starts massaging Bhabiji's back. She gives him her favourite blessing: 'God protect you and give you lots of children.' If God listens to all of Bhabiji's prayers and blessings, there will never be a fall in the population.

The lights are off and Bhabiji settles down for the night. She is almost asleep when a small voice pipes up: 'Bhabiji, tell us a story.'

At first Bhabiji pretends not to hear; then, when the request is repeated, she says: 'You'll keep Aunty Shobha awake, and then she'll have an excuse for getting up late in the morning.' But the children know Bhabiji's one great weakness, and they renew their demand.

'Your grandmother is tired,' says Arun. 'Let her sleep.'

But Bhabiji's eyes are open. Her mind is going back over the crowded years, and she remembers something very interesting that happened when her younger brother's wife's sister married the eldest son of her third cousin...

Before long, the children are asleep, and I am wondering if I will ever sleep, for Bhabiji's voice drones on, into the darker reaches of the night.

THE GREAT INDIAN ROPE TRICK

Everyone has heard of the great Indian rope trick, but I am probably the only person who has actually seen it performed.

It was many years ago, when I was wandering around in the small towns of North India, making a living by writing the occasional story or newspaper article, and staying in cheap hotels or small rented rooms.

I was visiting Kalsi, on the road to Chakrata, with the intention of writing a piece on the rock edicts of the great King Asoka, edicts that had survived in stone for thousands of years.

On a hillock nearby, a small but lively crowd had collected—mostly village folk from the surrounding farmlands—and, like most rustic folk, they were more interested in magic than in history. Come to think of it, so was I!

The object of their interest was a man in a mustard-coloured robe, accompanied by a skinny young boy wearing nothing but a loincloth, or *langoti*. With the help of his acolyte, the man had been performing various feats of magic, to the amusement of the gathering.

The magician claimed that he could invert the order of nature, and someone in the crowd challenged him to produce out of thin air a bunch of coconuts, well-knowing that coconuts grew by the sea and not in the Himalayan foothills.

'Well, you won't find coconuts growing here,' said the magician, 'but perhaps there are some to be found above the clouds, in the land of the Gods.'

'But how are we to fetch them?' asked the boy.

'I have the means,' said the man, and proceeded to take from a large round tin box, a cord some tens of feet in length. After carefully arranging the cord, he threw one end of it high up in the air—and there, to everyone's astonishment, it remained as if caught by something. He now paid out the corded rope, which kept going up higher and higher until it disappeared in the mist, leaving only a short length in his hands. He then told the crowd that as he was too heavy to climb the rope himself, he would ask the boy to do so. And handing the end of the rope to the boy, he told him to go ahead.

At first the boy demurred, saying that if he fell from a great height, he would surely be killed. But on being thumped on the head by his angry mentor, he seized the rope and swarmed up it, looking rather like a small spider running up a hanging thread from a wall.

In a few moments, the boy was out of sight, and the crowd fell silent, wondering what would happen next.

Presently, down fell a large coconut—a real coconut—which the pleased magician presented to someone in the crowd. It was followed by several more coconuts.

Then, suddenly, the rope came down, without the boy, and the magician shrieked, 'Someone has cut the rope! What will my boy do now?'

A minute later, down came the boy's head. It bounced on the ground, like a coconut.

This was followed by the boy's arms, legs and body, all falling to the ground one after another.

The mesmerized crowd had been watching these startling events in horror and amazement when suddenly the lid of the tin box flew open and the boy popped out and bowed to the crowd.

A cheer went up, and coins were thrown to the smiling performers. They thanked the crowd with folded hands.

How had they done this trick—if indeed it was a trick? Mesmerism, hypnotism, the powers of suggestion?

The coil of rope was back in its box; the fallen limbs were nowhere to be seen.

As the magician passed me, he smiled and held out a coconut, which I took in both hands. It seemed to quiver as I held it!

Then, as I looked down at the coconut, I saw it change into a human face. Two eyes looked out at me, and a wide mouth broke into a sly grin. This transformation lasted only for seconds, and then it was a coconut again.

I dropped the coconut. It rolled away, and was seized upon by several street urchins, who made off with it.

I turned to see if the magician was still around, and was just in time to catch a glimpse of the man and the boy and the tin box as they disappeared into the crowd—into the mystery and multitude that was India.

'LET'S GO TO THE PICTURES!'

My love affair with the cinema began when I was five and ended when I was about fifty. Not because I wanted it to, but because all my favourite cinema halls were closing down—being turned into shopping malls or garages or just disappearing altogether.

There was something magical about sitting in a darkened cinema hall, the audience silent, completely focused on the drama unfolding on the big screen. You could escape to a different world—run away to Dover with David Copperfield, sail away to a treasure island with Long John Silver, dance the light fantastic with Fred Astaire or Gene Kelly, sing with Saigal or Deanna Durbin or Nelson Eddy, fall in love with Madhubala or Elizabeth Taylor. And until the lights came on at the end of the show you were in their world, far removed from the troubles of one's own childhood or the struggles of early manhood.

Watching films on TV cannot be the same. People come and go, the power comes and goes, other viewers keep switching the channels, food is continually being served or consumed, family squabbles are ever present, and there is no escape from those dreaded commercials that are repeated every ten or fifteen minutes, or even between overs if you happen to be watching cricket.

No longer do we hear that evocative suggestion: 'Let's go to the pictures!'

Living in Mussoorie where there are no longer any functioning cinemas, the invitation is heard no more. I'm afraid there isn't half as much excitement in the words 'Let's put on the TV!'

For one thing, going to the pictures meant going out—on foot, or on a bicycle, or in the family car. When I lived on the outskirts of Mussoorie, it took me almost an hour to climb the hill into town to see a film at one of our tiny halls—but walk I did, in hot sun or drenching rain or icy wind, because going to the pictures was an event in itself, a break from more mundane activities, quite often a social occasion. You would meet friends from other parts of the town, and after the show you would join them in a cafe for a cup of tea and the latest gossip. A stroll along the Mall and a visit to the local bookshop would bring the evening to a satisfying end. A long walk home under the stars, a drink before dinner, something to listen to on the radio... 'And then to bed,' as Mr Pepys would have said.

Not that everything went smoothly in our small-town cinemas. In Shimla, Mussoorie and other hill stations, the roofs were of corrugated tin sheets, and when there was heavy rain or a hailstorm it would be impossible to hear the soundtrack. You had then to imagine that you were back in the silent film era.

Mussoorie's oldest cinema, the Picture Palace, did in fact open early in the silent era. This was in 1912, the year electricity came to the town. Later, its basement floor was also turned into a cinema, the Jubilee, which probably made it India's first multiplex hall. Sadly, both closed down about five years ago, along with the Rialto, the Majestic and the Capitol (below Halman's Hotel).

In Shimla, we had the Ritz, the Regal and the Rivoli. This was when I was a schoolboy at Bishop Cotton's. How we used to look forward to our summer and autumn breaks. We would be allowed into town during these holidays, and we lost no time in tramping up to the Ridge to take in the latest films. Sometimes we'd arrive wet or perspiring, but the changeable weather did not prevent us from enjoying the film. One-and-a-half hours escape from the routine and discipline of boarding school life. Fast foods had yet to be invented, but roasted peanuts or *bhutta*s would keep us going. They were cheap too. The cinema ticket was just over a rupee. If you had five rupees in your pocket you could enjoy a pleasant few hours in the town.

It was during the winter holidays—three months of time on my hands—that I really caught up with the films of the day.

New Delhi, the winter of 1943. Second World War was still in progress. The halls were flooded with British and American movies. My father would return from Air Headquarters, where he'd been working on cyphers all day. 'Let's go to the pictures,' he'd say, and we'd be off to the Regal or Rivoli or Odeon or Plaza, only a short walk from our rooms on Atul Grove Road.

Comedies were my favourites. Laurel and Hardy, Abbott and Costello, George Formby, Harold Lloyd, the Marx Brothers... And sometimes we'd venture further afield, to the old Ritz at Kashmere Gate, to see Sabu in *The Thief of Baghdad* or *Cobra Woman*. These *Arabian Nights*-type entertainments were popular in the old city.

The Statesman, the premier newspaper of that era, ran ads for all the films in town, and I'd cut them out and stick them in a scrapbook. I could rattle off the cast of all the pictures I'd seen, and today, sixty years later, I can still name all the actors (and sometimes the director) of almost every 1940s film.

My father died when I was ten and I went to live with my mother and stepfather in Dehradun. Dehra too, was well served with cinemas, but I was a lonely picturegoer. I had no friends or companions in those years, and I would trudge off on my own to the Orient or Odeon or Hollywood, to indulge in a few hours of escapism. Books were there, of course, providing another and better form of escape, but books had to be read in the home, and sometimes I wanted to get away from the house and pursue a solitary other-life in the anonymous privacy of a darkened cinema hall.

It has gone now, the little Odeon cinema opposite the old Parade Ground in Dehra. Many of my age, and younger, will remember it with affection, for it was probably the most popular meeting place for English cinema buffs in the '40s and '50s. You could get a good idea of the popularity of a film by looking at the number of bicycles ranged outside. Dehra was a bicycle town. The scooter hadn't been invented, and cars were few. I belonged to a minority of walkers. I have walked all over the towns and cities I have lived in—Dehradun, New and Old Delhi, London, St Helier (in Jersey) and our hill stations. Those walks often ended at the cinema!

The Odeon was a twenty-minute walk from the Old Survey Road, where we lived at the time, and after the evening show I would walk home across the deserted parade ground, the starry night adding to my dreams of a starry world, where tap dancers, singing cowboys, swashbuckling swordsmen and glamorous women in sarongs reigned supreme in the firmament. I wasn't just a daydreamer; I was a star-dreamer.

During the intervals (five-minute breaks between the shorts and the main feature), the projectionist or his assistant would play a couple of gramophone records for the benefit of the audience. Unfortunately, the management had only two or three records, and the audience would grow restless listening to the same tunes at every show. I must have been compelled to listen to 'Don't Fence Me In' about a hundred times, and felt thoroughly fenced in.

At home, I had a good collection of gramophone records, passed on to me by relatives and neighbours who were leaving India around the time of Independence. I decided it would be a good idea to give some of them to the cinema's management so that we could be provided with a little more variety during the intervals. I made a selection of about twenty records—mostly dance music of the period—and presented them to the manager, Mr Suri.

Mr Suri was delighted. And to show me his gratitude, he presented me with a Free Pass that permitted me to see all the pictures I liked without having to buy a ticket! Any day, any show, for as long as Mr Suri was the manager! Could any ardent picturegoer have asked for more?

This unexpected bonanza lasted for almost two years with the result that during my school holidays, I saw a film every second day. Two days was the average run for most films. Except *Gone With the Wind,* which ran for a week, to my great chagrin. I found it so boring that I left in the middle.

Usually I did enjoy films based on famous or familiar books. Dickens was a natural for the screen. *David Copperfield, Oliver Twist, Great Expectations, Nicholas Nickleby, A Tale of Two Cities, Pickwick Papers, A Christmas Carol,* all made successful films, true to the originals. Daphne du Maurier's novels also transferred well to the screen. As did Somerset Maugham's works: *Of Human Bondage, The Razor's Edge, The Letter, Rain,* and several others.

Occasionally I brought the management a change of records. Mr Suri was not a very communicative man, but I think he liked me (he knew something about my circumstances) and with a smile and a wave of the hand he would indicate that the freedom of the hall was mine.

Eventually, school finished, I was packed off to England, where my picture-going days went into a slight decline. No Free Passes any more. But on Jersey island, where I lived and worked for a year, I found an out-of-the-way cinema that specialized in showing old comedies, and here I caught up with many British film comedians such as Tommy Trinder, Sidney Howard, Max

Miller, Will Hay, Old Mother Riley (a man in reality) and Gracie Fields. These artistes had been but names to me, as their films had never come to India. I was thrilled to be able to discover and enjoy their considerable talents. You would be hard put to find their films today; they have seldom been revived.

In London for two years I had an office job and most of my spare time was spent in writing (and rewriting) my first novel. All the same, I took to the streets and discovered the Everyman cinema in Hampstead, which showed old classics, including the films of Jean Renoir and Orson Welles. And the Academy in Leicester Square, which showed the best films from the continent. I also discovered a couple of seedy little cinemas in the East End, which appropriately showed the early gangster films of James Cagney and Humphrey Bogart.

I also saw the first Indian film to get a regular screening in London. It was called *Aan,* and was the usual extravagant mix of music and melodrama. But it ran for two or three weeks. Homesick Indians (which included me) flocked to see it. One of its stars was Nadira, who specialized in playing the scheming sultry villainess. A few years ago, she came out of retirement to take the part of Miss Mackenzie in a TV serial based on some of my short stories set in Mussoorie. A sympathetic role for a change. And she played it to perfection.

It was four years before I saw Dehra again. Mr Suri had gone elsewhere. The little cinema had closed down and was about to be demolished, to make way for a hotel and a block of shops.

We must move on, of course. There's no point in hankering after distant pleasures and lost picture palaces. But there's no harm in indulging in a little nostalgia. What is nostalgia, after all, but an attempt to preserve that which was good in the past?

And last year I was reminded of that golden era of the silver screen. I was rummaging around in a *kabari* shop in one of Dehradun's bazaars where I came across a pile of old 78 RPM records, all looking a little the worse for wear. And on a couple of them I found my name scratched on the labels. 'Pennies from Heaven' was the title of one of the songs. It had certainly saved me a few rupees. That and the goodwill of Mr Suri, the Odeon's manager, all those years ago.

I bought the records. Can't play them now. No wind-up gramophone! But I am a sentimental fellow and I keep them among my souvenirs as a reminder of the days when I walked home alone across the silent, moonlit parade ground, after the evening show was over.

MUKESH STARTS A ZOO

On a visit to Delhi with his parents, Mukesh spent two crowded hours at the zoo. He was dazzled by the many colourful birds, fascinated by the reptiles, charmed by the gibbons and chimps, and awestruck by the big cats—the lions, tigers and leopards. There was no zoo in the small town of Dehra where he lived, and the jungle was some way across the river-bed. So, as soon as he got home, he decided that he would have a zoo of his own.

'I'm going to start a zoo,' he announced at breakfast, the day after his return.

'But you don't have any birds or animals,' said Dolly, his little sister.

'I'll soon find them,' said Mukesh. 'That's what a zoo is all about—collecting animals.'

He was gazing at the white-washed walls of the verandah, where a gecko, a small wall lizard, was in pursuit of a fly. A little later Mukesh was trying to catch the lizard. But it was more alert than it looked, and always managed to keep a few inches ahead of his grasp.

'That's not the way to catch a lizard,' said Teju, appearing on the verandah steps. Teju and his sister Koki lived next door.

'You catch it, then,' said Mukesh.

Teju fetched a stick from the garden, where it had been used to prop up sweet-peas. He used the stick to tip the lizard off the wall and into a shoe-box.

'You'll be my Head Keeper,' said Mukesh, and soon he and Teju were at work in the back garden setting up enclosures with a roll of wire-netting they had found in the poultry shed.

'What else can we have in the zoo?' asked Teju. 'We need more than a lizard.'

'There's your grandmother's parrot,' said Mukesh.

'That's a good idea. But we won't tell her about it—not yet. I don't think she'd lend it to us. You see, it's a *religious* parrot. She's taught it lots of prayers and chants.'

'Then people are sure to come and listen to it. They'll pay, too.'

'We must have the parrot, then. What else?'

'Well, there's my dog,' said Mukesh. 'He's very fierce.'

'But a dog isn't a zoo animal.'

'Mine is—he's a wild dog. Look, he's black all over and he's got yellow eyes. There's no other dog like him.'

Mukesh's dog, who spent most of his time sleeping on the verandah, raised his head and obligingly revealed his yellow eyes.

'He's got jaundice,' said Teju. 'They've always been yellow.'

'All right, then, we've got a lizard, a parrot and a black dog with yellow eyes.'

'Koki has a white rabbit. Will she lend it to us?'

'I don't know. She thinks a lot of her rabbit. Maybe we can rent it from her.'

'And there's Sitaram's donkey.'

Sitaram, the dhobi-boy, usually used a donkey to deliver and collect the laundry from the houses along this particular street.

'Do you really want a donkey?' asked Teju doubtfully.

'Why not? It's a wild donkey. Haven't you heard of them?'

'I've heard of a wild ass, but not a wild donkey.'

'Well, they're all related to each other—asses, donkeys and mules.'

'Why don't you paint black stripes on it and call it a zebra?'

'No, that's cheating. It's got to be a proper zoo. No tricks—it's not a circus!'

On Saturday afternoon, a large placard with corrected spelling announced the opening of the zoo. It hung from the branches of the jack-fruit tree. Children were allowed in free but grown-ups had to buy tickets at fifty paise each, and Koki and Dolly were selling home-made tickets to the occasional passer-by or parent who happened to look in. Mukesh and his friends had worked hard at making notices for the various enclosures and each resident of the zoo was appropriately named.

The first attraction was a large packing-case filled with an assortment of house-lizards. They looked rather sluggish, having been generously fed with a supply of beetles and other insects.

Then came an enclosure in which Koki's white rabbit was on display. Freshly washed and brushed, it looked very cuddly and was praised by all.

Staring at it with evil intent from behind wire-netting was Mukesh's dog—RARE BLACK DOG WITH YELLOW EYES read the notice. Those yellow eyes were now trying hard to hypnotize the pink eyes of Koki's nervous rabbit. The dog pawed at the ground, trying to dig its way out from under the fence to get at the rabbit.

Tethered to a mango tree was Sitaram's small donkey. And tacked to the tree was a placard saying WILD ASS FROM KUTCH. A distant relative it may have been, but everyone recognized it as the local washerman's beast of burden. Every now and then it tried to break loose, for it was long past its feeding time.

There was also a duck that did not seem to belong to anyone, and a small cow that had strayed in on its own; but the star attraction was the parrot. As it could recite three different prayers, over and over again, it was soon surrounded by a group of admiring parents, all of whom wished they had a parrot who could pray, or rather, do their praying for them.

Oddly enough, Koki's grandmother had chosen that day for visiting the temple, so she was unaware of the fuss that was being made of her pet, or even that it had been made an honorary member of the zoo. Teju had convinced himself she wouldn't mind.

While Mukesh and Teju were escorting visitors around the zoo, lecturing them on wild dogs and wild asses, Koki and Dolly were doing a brisk trade at the ticket counter. They had collected about ten rupees and were hoping for yet more, when there was a disturbance in the enclosures.

The black dog with yellow eyes had finally managed to dig his way out of his cage, and was now busy trying to dig his way into the rabbit's compartment. The rabbit was running round and round in panic-stricken circles. Meanwhile, the donkey had finally snapped the rope that held it and, braying loudly, scattered the spectators and made for home.

Koki went to the rescue of her rabbit and soon had it cradled in her arms. The dog now turned his attention to the duck. The duck flew over the packing-case, while the dog landed in it, scattering lizards in all directions.

In all this confusion, no one noticed that the door of the parrot's cage had slipped open. With a squawk and a whirr of wings, the bird shot out of the cage and flew off into a nearby orchard.

'The parrot's gone!' shouted Dolly, and almost immediately a silence fell upon the assembled visitors and children. Even the dog stopped barking. Granny's praying parrot had escaped! How could they possibly face her? Teju wondered if she would believe him if he told her it had flown off to heaven.

'Can anyone see it?' he asked tearfully.

'It's in a mango tree,' said Dolly. 'It won't come back.'

The crowd fell away, unwilling to share any of the blame

when Koki's grandmother came home and discovered what had happened.

'What are we going to do now?' asked Teju, looking to Koki for help; but Koki was too upset to suggest anything. Mukesh had an idea.

'I know!' he said. 'We'll get another one!'

'How?'

'Well, there's the ten rupees we've collected. We can buy a new parrot for ten rupees!'

'But won't Granny know the difference?' asked Teju.

'All these hill parrots look alike,' said Mukesh.

So, taking the cage with them, they hurried off to the bazaar, where they soon found a bird-seller who was happy to sell them a parrot not unlike Granny's. He assured them it would talk.

'It looks like your grandmother's parrot,' said Mukesh on the way home. 'But can it pray?'

'Of course not,' said Koki. 'But we can teach it.'

Koki's grandmother, who was short-sighted, did not notice the substitution; but she complained bitterly that the bird had stopped repeating its prayers and was instead making rude noises and even swearing occasionally.

Teju soon remedied this sad state of affairs.

Every morning he stood in front of the parrot's cage and repeated Granny's prayers. Within a few weeks the bird had learnt to repeat one of them. Granny was happy again—not only because her parrot had started praying once more, but because Teju had started praying too!

THE BLUE UMBRELLA

I

'Neelu! Neelu!' cried Binya.

She scrambled barefoot over the rocks, ran over the short summer grass, up and over the brow of the hill, all the time calling 'Neelu, Neelu!' Neelu—Blue—was the name of the blue-grey cow. The other cow, which was white, was called Gori, meaning Fair One. They were fond of wandering off on their own, down to the stream or into the pine forest, and sometimes they came back by themselves and sometimes they stayed away—almost deliberately, it seemed to Binya.

If the cows didn't come home at the right time, Binya would be sent to fetch them. Sometimes her brother, Bijju, went with her, but these days he was busy preparing for his exams and didn't have time to help with the cows.

Binya liked being on her own, and sometimes she allowed the cows to lead her into some distant valley, and then they would all be late coming home. The cows preferred having Binya with them, because she let them wander. Bijju pulled them by their tails if they went too far.

Binya belonged to the mountains, to this part of the Himalaya known as Garhwal. Dark forests and lonely hilltops held no terrors for her. It was only when she was in the market town, jostled by the crowds in the bazaar, that she felt rather nervous and lost. The town, five miles from the village, was also a pleasure resort for tourists from all over India.

Binya was probably ten. She may have been nine or even

eleven, she couldn't be sure because no one in the village kept birthdays; but her mother told her she'd been born during a winter when the snow had come up to the windows, and that was just over ten years ago, wasn't it? Two years later, her father had died, but his passing had made no difference to their way of life. They had three tiny terraced fields on the side of the mountain, and they grew potatoes, onions, ginger, beans, mustard and maize: not enough to sell in the town, but enough to live on.

Like most mountain girls, Binya was quite sturdy, fair of skin, with pink cheeks and dark eyes and her black hair tied in a pigtail. She wore pretty glass bangles on her wrists, and a necklace of glass beads. From the necklace hung a leopard's claw. It was a lucky charm, and Binya always wore it. Bijju had one, too, only his was attached to a string.

Binya's full name was Binyadevi, and Bijju's real name was Vijay, but everyone called them Binya and Bijju. Binya was two years younger than her brother.

She had stopped calling for Neelu; she had heard the cowbells tinkling, and knew the cows hadn't gone far. Singing to herself, she walked over fallen pine needles into the forest glade on the spur of the hill. She heard voices, laughter, the clatter of plates and cups, and stepping through the trees, she came upon a party of picnickers.

They were holidaymakers from the plains. The women were dressed in bright saris, the men wore light summer shirts and the children had pretty new clothes. Binya, standing in the shadows between the trees, went unnoticed; for some time she watched the picnickers, admiring their clothes, listening to their unfamiliar accents and gazing rather hungrily at the sight of all their food. And then her gaze came to rest on a bright blue umbrella, a frilly thing for women, which lay open on the grass beside its owner.

Now Binya had seen umbrellas before, and her mother had

a big black umbrella that nobody used anymore because the field rats had eaten holes in it, but this was the first time Binya had seen such a small, dainty, colourful umbrella and she fell in love with it. The umbrella was like a flower, a great blue flower that had sprung up on the dry brown hillside.

She moved forward a few paces so that she could see the umbrella better. As she came out of the shadows into the sunlight, the picnickers saw her.

'Hello, look who's here!' exclaimed the older of the two women. 'A little village girl!'

'Isn't she pretty?' remarked the other. 'But how torn and dirty her clothes are!' It did not seem to bother them that Binya could hear and understand everything they said about her.

'They're very poor in the hills,' said one of the men.

'Then let's give her something to eat.' And the older woman beckoned to Binya to come closer.

Hesitantly, nervously, Binya approached the group.

Normally she would have turned and fled, but the attraction was the pretty blue umbrella. It had cast a spell over her, drawing her forward almost against her will.

'What's that on her neck?' asked the younger woman.

'A necklace of sorts.'

'It's a pendant—see, there's a claw hanging from it!'

'It's a tiger's claw,' said the man beside her. (He had never seen a tiger's claw.) 'A lucky charm. These people wear them to keep away evil spirits.' He looked to Binya for confirmation, but Binya said nothing.

'Oh, I want one too!' said the woman, who was obviously his wife.

'You can't get them in shops.'

'Buy hers, then. Give her two or three rupees, she's sure to need the money.'

The man, looking slightly embarrassed but anxious to please his young wife, produced a two-rupee note and offered it to Binya, indicating that he wanted the pendant in exchange. Binya put her hand to the necklace, half afraid that the excited woman would snatch it away from her. Solemnly she shook her head.

The man then showed her a five-rupee note, but again Binya shook her head.

'How silly she is!' exclaimed the young woman.

'It may not be hers to sell,' said the man. 'But I'll try again. How much do you want—what can we give you?' And he waved his hand towards the picnic things scattered about on the grass.

Without any hesitation Binya pointed to the umbrella.

'My umbrella!' exclaimed the young woman. 'She wants my umbrella. What cheek!'

'Well, you want her pendant, don't you?'

'That's different.'

'Is it?'

The man and his wife were beginning to quarrel with each other.

'I'll ask her to go away,' said the older woman. 'We're making such fools of ourselves.'

'But I want the pendant!' cried the other, petulantly.

And then, on an impulse, she picked up the umbrella and held it out to Binya.

'Here, take the umbrella!'

Binya removed her necklace and held it out to the young woman, who immediately placed it around her own neck. Then Binya took the umbrella and held it up. It did not look so small in her hands; in fact, it was just the right size.

She had forgotten about the picnickers, who were busy examining the pendant. She turned the blue umbrella this way and that, looked through the bright blue silk at the pulsating

sun, and then, still keeping it open, turned and disappeared
into the forest glade.

II

Binya seldom closed the blue umbrella. Even when she had it
in the house, she left it lying open in a corner of the room.
Sometimes Bijju snapped it shut, complaining that it got in the
way. She would open it again a little later. It wasn't beautiful
when it was closed.

Whenever Binya went out—whether it was to graze the
cows, or fetch water from the spring, or carry milk to the little
tea shop on the Tehri road—she took the umbrella with her.
That patch of sky blue silk could always be seen on the hillside.

Old Ram Bharosa (Ram the Trustworthy) kept the tea shop
on the Tehri road. It was a dusty, un-metalled road. Once a
day, the Tehri bus stopped near his shop and passengers got
down to sip hot tea or drink a glass of curd. He kept a few
bottles of Coca-Cola too, but as there was no ice, the bottles
got hot in the sun and so were seldom opened. He also kept
sweets and toffees, and when Binya or Bijju had a few coins
to spare, they would spend them at the shop. It was only a
mile from the village.

Ram Bharosa was astonished to see Binya's blue umbrella.
'What have you there, Binya?' he asked.

Binya gave the umbrella a twirl and smiled at Ram Bharosa.
She was always ready with her smile, and would willingly have
lent it to anyone who was feeling unhappy.

'That's a lady's umbrella,' said Ram Bharosa. 'That's only
for memsahibs. Where did you get it?'

'Someone gave it to me—for my necklace.'

'You exchanged it for your lucky claw!'

Binya nodded.

'But what do you need it for? The sun isn't hot enough, and it isn't meant for the rain. It's just a pretty thing for rich ladies to play with!'

Binya nodded and smiled again. Ram Bharosa was quite right; it was just a beautiful plaything. And that was exactly why she had fallen in love with it.

'I have an idea,' said the shopkeeper. 'It's no use to you, that umbrella. Why not sell it to me? I'll give you five rupees for it.'

'It's worth fifteen,' said Binya.

'Well, then, I'll give you ten.'

Binya laughed and shook her head.

'Twelve rupees?' said Ram Bharosa, but without much hope.

Binya placed a five-paise coin on the counter.

'I came for a toffee,' she said.

Ram Bharosa pulled at his drooping whiskers, gave Binya a wry look, and placed a toffee in the palm of her hand. He watched Binya as she walked away along the dusty road. The blue umbrella held him fascinated, and he stared after it until it was out of sight.

The villagers used this road to go to the market town. Some used the bus, a few rode on mules and most people walked. Today, everyone on the road turned their heads to stare at the girl with the bright blue umbrella.

Binya sat down in the shade of a pine tree. The umbrella, still open, lay beside her. She cradled her head in her arms, and presently she dozed off. It was that kind of day, sleepily warm and summery.

And while she slept, a wind sprang up.

It came quietly, swishing gently through the trees, humming softly. Then it was joined by other random gusts, bustling over the tops of the mountains. The trees shook their heads and came to life. The wind fanned Binya's cheeks. The umbrella stirred on the grass.

The wind grew stronger, picking up dead leaves and sending them spinning and swirling through the air. It got into the umbrella and began to drag it over the grass. Suddenly it lifted the umbrella and carried it about six feet from the sleeping girl. The sound woke Binya.

She was on her feet immediately, and then she was leaping down the steep slope. But just as she was within reach of the umbrella, the wind picked it up again and carried it further downhill.

Binya set off in pursuit. The wind was in a wicked, playful mood. It would leave the umbrella alone for a few moments but as soon as Binya came near, it would pick up the umbrella again and send it bouncing, floating, dancing away from her.

The hill grew steeper. Binya knew that after twenty yards it would fall away in a precipice. She ran faster. And the wind ran with her, ahead of her, and the blue umbrella stayed up with the wind.

A fresh gust picked it up and carried it to the very edge of the cliff. There it balanced for a few seconds, before toppling over, out of sight.

Binya ran to the edge of the cliff. Going down on her hands and knees, she peered down the cliff face. About a hundred feet below, a small stream rushed between great boulders. Hardly anything grew on the cliff face—just a few stunted bushes, and, halfway down, a wild cherry tree growing crookedly out of the rocks and hanging across the chasm. The umbrella had stuck in the cherry tree.

Binya didn't hesitate. She may have been timid with strangers, but she was at home on a hillside. She stuck her bare leg over the edge of the cliff and began climbing down. She kept her face to the hillside, feeling her way with her feet, only changing her handhold when she knew her feet were secure.

Sometimes she held on to the thorny bilberry bushes, but she did not trust the other plants, which came away very easily.

Loose stones rattled down the cliff. Once on their way, the stones did not stop until they reached the bottom of the hill; and they took other stones with them, so that there was soon a cascade of stones, and Binya had to be very careful not to start a landslide.

As agile as a mountain goat, she did not take more than five minutes to reach the crooked cherry tree. But the most difficult task remained—she had to crawl along the trunk of the tree, which stood out at right angles from the cliff. Only by doing this could she reach the trapped umbrella.

Binya felt no fear when climbing trees. She was proud of the fact that she could climb them as well as Bijju. Gripping the rough cherry bark with her toes, and using her knees as leverage, she crawled along the trunk of the projecting tree until she was almost within reach of the umbrella. She noticed with dismay that the blue cloth was torn in a couple of places.

She looked down, and it was only then that she felt afraid. She was right over the chasm, balanced precariously about eighty feet above the boulder-strewn stream. Looking down, she felt quite dizzy. Her hands shook, and the tree shook too. If she slipped now, there was only one direction in which she could fall—down, down, into the depths of that dark and shadowy ravine.

There was only one thing to do; concentrate on the patch of blue just a couple of feet away from her. She did not look down or up, but straight ahead, and willing herself forward, she managed to reach the umbrella.

She could not crawl back with it in her hands. So, after dislodging it from the forked branch in which it had stuck, she let it fall, still open, into the ravine below.

Cushioned by the wind, the umbrella floated serenely downwards, landing in a thicket of nettles.

Binya crawled back along the trunk of the cherry tree. Twenty minutes later, she emerged from the nettle clump, her precious umbrella held aloft. She had nettle stings all over her legs, but she was hardly aware of the smarting. She was as immune to nettles as Bijju was to bees.

III

About four years previously, Bijju had knocked a hive out of an oak tree, and had been badly stung on the face and legs. It had been a painful experience. But now, if a bee stung him, he felt nothing at all: he had been immunized for life!

He was on his way home from school. It was two o'clock and he hadn't eaten since six in the morning. Fortunately, the kingora bushes—the bilberries—were in fruit, and already Bijju's lips were stained purple with the juice of the wild, sour fruit.

He didn't have any money to spend at Ram Bharosa's shop, but he stopped there anyway to look at the sweets in their glass jars.

'And what will you have today?' asked Ram Bharosa.

'No money,' said Bijju.

'You can pay me later.'

Bijju shook his head. Some of his friends had taken sweets on credit, and at the end of the month they had found they'd eaten more sweets than they could possibly pay for! As a result, they'd had to hand over to Ram Bharosa some of their most treasured possessions—such as a curved knife for cutting grass or a small hand-axe or a jar for pickles or a pair of earrings—and these had become the shopkeeper's possessions and were kept by him or sold in his shop.

Ram Bharosa had set his heart on having Binya's blue

umbrella, and so naturally he was anxious to give credit to either of the children, but so far neither had fallen into the trap.

Bijju moved on, his mouth full of Kingora berries. Halfway home, he saw Binya with the cows. It was late evening, and the sun had gone down, but Binya still had the umbrella open. The two small rents had been stitched up by her mother.

Bijju gave his sister a handful of berries. She handed him the umbrella while she ate the berries.

'You can have the umbrella until we get home,' she said. It was her way of rewarding Bijju for bringing her the wild fruit.

Calling 'Neelu! Gori!' Binya and Bijju set out for home, followed at some distance by the cows.

It was dark before they reached the village, but Bijju still had the umbrella open.

◆

Most of the people in the village were a little envious of Binya's blue umbrella. No one else had ever possessed one like it. The schoolmaster's wife thought it was quite wrong for a poor cultivator's daughter to have such a fine umbrella while she, a second-class BA, had to make do with an ordinary black one. Her husband offered to have their old umbrella dyed blue; she gave him a scornful look, and loved him a little less than before. The pujari, who looked after the temple, announced that he would buy a multi-coloured umbrella the next time he was in the town. A few days later he returned looking annoyed and grumbling that they weren't available except in Delhi. Most people consoled themselves by saying that Binya's pretty umbrella wouldn't keep out the rain, if it rained heavily; that it would shrivel in the sun, if the sun was fierce; that it would collapse in a wind, if the wind was strong; that it would attract lightning, if lightning fell near it; and that it would prove unlucky, if there was any ill luck going about. Secretly, everyone admired it.

Unlike the adults, the children didn't have to pretend. They were full of praise for the umbrella. It was so light, so pretty, so bright a blue! And it was just the right size for Binya. They knew that if they said nice things about the umbrella, Binya would smile and give it to them to hold for a little while—just a very little while!

Soon it was the time of the monsoon. Big black clouds kept piling up, and thunder rolled over the hills.

Binya sat on the hillside all afternoon, waiting for the rain. As soon as the first big drop of rain came down, she raised the umbrella over her head. More drops, big ones, came pattering down. She could see them through the umbrella silk, as they broke against the cloth.

And then there was a cloudburst, and it was like standing under a waterfall. The umbrella wasn't really a rain umbrella, but it held up bravely. Only Binya's feet got wet. Rods of rain fell around her in a curtain of shivered glass.

Everywhere on the hillside people were scurrying for shelter. Some made for a charcoal burner's hut, others for a mule-shed, or Ram Bharosa's shop. Binya was the only one who didn't run. This was what she'd been waiting for—rain on her umbrella—and she wasn't in a hurry to go home. She didn't mind getting her feet wet. The cows didn't mind getting wet either.

Presently she found Bijju sheltering in a cave. He would have enjoyed getting wet, but he had his schoolbooks with him and he couldn't afford to let them get spoilt. When he saw Binya, he came out of the cave and shared the umbrella. He was a head taller than his sister, so he had to hold the umbrella for her, while she held his books.

The cows had been left far behind.

'Neelu, Neelu!' called Binya.

'Gori!' called Bijju.

When their mother saw them sauntering home through the driving rain, she called out: 'Binya! Bijju! Hurry up, and bring the cows in! What are you doing out there in the rain?'

'Just testing the umbrella,' said Bijju.

IV

The rains set in, and the sun only made brief appearances. The hills turned a lush green. Ferns sprang up on walls and tree trunks. Giant lilies reared up like leopards from the tall grass. A white mist coiled and uncoiled as it floated up from the valley. It was a beautiful season, except for the leeches.

Every day, Binya came home with a couple of leeches fastened to the flesh of her bare legs. They fell off by themselves just as soon as they'd had their thimbleful of blood, but you didn't know they were on you until they fell off, and then, later, the skin became very sore and itchy. Some of the older people still believed that to be bled by leeches was a remedy for various ailments. Whenever Ram Bharosa had a headache, he applied a leech to his throbbing temple.

Three days of incessant rain had flooded out a number of small animals who lived in holes in the ground. Binya's mother suddenly found the roof full of field rats. She had to drive them out; they ate too much of her stored-up wheat flour and rice. Bijju liked lifting up large rocks to disturb the scorpions who were sleeping beneath. And snakes came out to bask in the sun.

Binya had just crossed the small stream at the bottom of the hill when she saw something gliding out of the bushes and coming towards her. It was a long black snake. A clatter of loose stones frightened it. Seeing the girl in its way, it rose up, hissing, prepared to strike. The forked tongue darted out, the venomous head lunged at Binya.

Binya's umbrella was open as usual. She thrust it forward, between herself and the snake, and the snake's hard snout thudded twice against the strong silk of the umbrella. The reptile then turned and slithered away over the wet rocks, disappearing into a clump of ferns.

Binya forgot about the cows and ran all the way home to tell her mother how she had been saved by the umbrella. Bijju had to put away his books and go out to fetch the cows. He carried a stout stick, in case he met with any snakes.

◆

First the summer sun, and now the endless rain, meant that the umbrella was beginning to fade a little. From a bright blue it had changed to a light blue. But it was still a pretty thing, and tougher than it looked, and Ram Bharosa still desired it. He did not want to sell it; he wanted to own it. He was probably the richest man in the area—so why shouldn't he have a blue umbrella? Not a day passed without his getting a glimpse of Binya and the umbrella; and the more he saw the umbrella, the more he wanted it.

The schools closed during the monsoon, but this didn't mean that Bijju could sit at home doing nothing. Neelu and Gori were providing more milk than was required at home, so Binya's mother was able to sell a kilo of milk every day: half a kilo to the schoolmaster, and half a kilo (at reduced rate) to the temple pujari. Bijju had to deliver the milk every morning.

Ram Bharosa had asked Bijju to work in his shop during the holidays, but Bijju didn't have time—he had to help his mother with the ploughing and the transplanting of the rice seedlings. So Ram Bharosa employed a boy from the next village, a boy called Rajaram. He did all the washing-up, and ran various errands. He went to the same school as Bijju, but the two boys were not friends.

One day, as Binya passed the shop, twirling her blue umbrella, Rajaram noticed that his employer gave a deep sigh and began muttering to himself.

'What's the matter, Babuji?' asked the boy.

'Oh, nothing,' said Ram Bharosa. 'It's just a sickness that has come upon me. And it's all due to that girl Binya and her wretched umbrella.'

'Why, what has she done to you?'

'Refused to sell me her umbrella! There's pride for you. And I offered her ten rupees.'

'Perhaps, if you gave her twelve…'

'But it isn't new any longer. It isn't worth eight rupees now. All the same, I'd like to have it.'

'You wouldn't make a profit on it,' said Rajaram.

'It's not the profit I'm after, wretch! It's the thing itself. It's the beauty of it!'

'And what would you do with it, Babuji? You don't visit anyone—you're seldom out of your shop. Of what use would it be to you?'

'Of what use is a poppy in a cornfield? Of what use is a rainbow? Of what use are you, numbskull? Wretch! I, too, have a soul. I want the umbrella, because—because I want its beauty to be mine!'

Rajaram put the kettle on to boil, began dusting the counter, all the time muttering: 'I'm as useful as an umbrella,' and then, after a short period of intense thought, said: 'What will you give me, Babuji, if I get the umbrella for you?'

'What do you mean?' asked the old man.

'You know what I mean. What will you give me?'

'You mean to steal it, don't you, you wretch? What a

delightful child you are! I'm glad you're not my son or my enemy. But look, everyone will know it has been stolen, and then how will I be able to show off with it?'

'You will have to gaze upon it in secret,' said Rajaram with a chuckle. 'Or take it into Tehri, and have it coloured red! That's your problem. But tell me, Babuji, do you want it badly enough to pay me three rupees for stealing it without being seen?'

Ram Bharosa gave the boy a long, sad look. 'You're a sharp boy,' he said. 'You'll come to a bad end. I'll give you two rupees.'

'Three,' said the boy.

'Two,' said the old man.

'You don't really want it, I can see that,' said the boy.

'Wretch!' said the old man. 'Evil one! Darkener of my doorstep! Fetch me the umbrella, and I'll give you three rupees.'

V

Binya was in the forest glade where she had first seen the umbrella. No one came there for picnics during the monsoon. The grass was always wet and the pine needles were slippery underfoot. The tall trees shut out the light, and poisonous-looking mushrooms, orange and purple, sprang up everywhere. But it was a good place for porcupines, who seemed to like the mushrooms, and Binya was searching for porcupine quills.

The hill people didn't think much of porcupine quills, but far away in southern India, the quills were valued as charms and sold at a rupee each. So Ram Bharosa paid a tenth of a rupee for each quill brought to him, and he in turn sold the quills at a profit to a trader from the plains.

Binya had already found five quills, and she knew there'd be more in the long grass. For once, she'd put her umbrella down. She had to put it aside if she was to search the ground thoroughly.

It was Rajaram's chance.

He'd been following Binya for some time, concealing himself behind trees and rocks, creeping closer whenever she became absorbed in her search. He was anxious that she should not see him and be able to recognize him later.

He waited until Binya had wandered some distance from the umbrella. Then, running forward at a crouch, he seized the open umbrella and dashed off with it.

But Rajaram had very big feet. Binya heard his heavy footsteps and turned just in time to see him as he disappeared between the trees. She cried out, dropped the porcupine quills, and gave chase.

Binya was swift and sure-footed, but Rajaram had a long stride. All the same, he made the mistake of running downhill. A long-legged person is much faster going uphill than down. Binya reached the edge of the forest glade in time to see the thief scrambling down the path to the stream. He had closed the umbrella so that it would not hinder his flight.

Binya was beginning to gain on the boy. He kept to the path, while she simply slid and leapt down the steep hillside. Near the bottom of the hill the path began to straighten out, and it was here that the long-legged boy began to forge ahead again.

Bijju was coming home from another direction. He had a bundle of sticks that he'd collected for the kitchen fire. As he reached the path, he saw Binya rushing down the hill as though all the mountain spirits in Garhwal were after her.

'What's wrong?' he called. 'Why are you running?'

Binya paused only to point at the fleeing Rajaram.

'My umbrella!' she cried. 'He has stolen it!'

Bijju dropped his bundle of sticks, and ran after his sister. When he reached her side, he said, 'I'll soon catch him!' and went sprinting away over the lush green grass. He was fresh, and he was soon well ahead of Binya and gaining on the thief.

Rajaram was crossing the shallow stream when Bijju caught up with him. Rajaram was the taller boy, but Bijju was much stronger. He flung himself at the thief, caught him by the legs, and brought him down in the water. Rajaram got to his feet and tried to drag himself away, but Bijju still had him by a leg. Rajaram overbalanced and came down with a great splash. He had let the umbrella fall. It began to float away on the current. Just then Binya arrived, flushed and breathless, and went dashing into the stream after the umbrella.

Meanwhile, a tremendous fight was taking place. Locked in fierce combat, the two boys swayed together on a rock, tumbled on to the sand, rolled over and over the pebbled bank until they were again thrashing about in the shallows of the stream. The magpies, bulbuls and other birds were disturbed, and flew away with cries of alarm.

Covered with mud, gasping and spluttering, the boys groped for each other in the water. After five minutes of frenzied struggle, Bijju emerged victorious.

Rajaram lay flat on his back on the sand, exhausted, while Bijju sat astride him, pinning him down with his arms and legs.

'Let me get up!' gasped Rajaram. 'Let me go—I don't want your useless umbrella!'

'Then why did you take it?' demanded Bijju. 'Come on—tell me why!'

'It was that skinflint Ram Bharosa,' said Rajaram.

'He told me to get it for him. He said if I didn't fetch it, I'd lose my job.'

◆

By early October, the rains were coming to an end. The leeches disappeared. The ferns turned yellow, and the sunlight on the green hills was mellow and golden, like the limes on the small tree in front of Binya's home. Bijju's days were happy ones as he came home from school, munching on roasted corn. Binya's umbrella had turned a pale milky blue, and was patched in several places, but it was still the prettiest umbrella in the village, and she still carried it with her wherever she went.

The cold, cruel winter wasn't far off, but somehow October seems longer than other months, because it is a kind month: the grass is good to be upon, the breeze is warm and gentle and pine-scented. That October, everyone seemed contented—everyone, that is, except Ram Bharosa.

The old man had by now given up all hope of ever possessing Binya's umbrella. He wished he had never set eyes on it. Because of the umbrella, he had suffered the tortures of greed, the despair of loneliness. Because of the umbrella, people had stopped coming to his shop!

Ever since it had become known that Ram Bharosa had tried to have the umbrella stolen, the village people had turned against him. They stopped trusting the old man; instead of buying their soap and tea and matches from his shop, they preferred to walk an extra mile to the shops near the Tehri bus stand. Who would have dealings with a man who had sold his soul for an umbrella? The children taunted him, twisted his name around. From 'Ram the Trustworthy' he became 'Trusty Umbrella Thief'.

The old man sat alone in his empty shop, listening to the eternal hissing of his kettle and wondering if anyone would ever again step in for a glass of tea. Ram Bharosa had lost his own appetite, and ate and drank very little. There was no money coming in. He had his savings in a bank in Tehri, but it was a terrible thing to have to dip into them! To save money, he had dismissed the blundering Rajaram. So he was left without any company. The roof leaked and the wind got in through the corrugated tin sheets, but Ram Bharosa didn't care.

Bijju and Binya passed his shop almost every day. Bijju went by with a loud but tuneless whistle. He was one of the world's whistlers; cares rested lightly on his shoulders. But, strangely enough, Binya crept quietly past the shop, looking the other way, almost as though she was in some way responsible for the misery of Ram Bharosa.

She kept reasoning with herself, telling herself that the umbrella was her very own, and that she couldn't help it if others were jealous of it. But had she loved the umbrella too much? Had it mattered more to her than people mattered? She couldn't help feeling that, in a small way, she was the cause of the sad look on Ram Bharosa's face ('His face is a yard long,' said Bijju) and the ruinous condition of his shop. It was all due to his own greed, no doubt, but she didn't want him to feel too bad about what he'd done, because it made her feel bad about herself; and so she closed the umbrella whenever she came near the shop, opening it again only when she was out of sight.

One day towards the end of October, when she had ten paise in her pocket, she entered the shop and asked the old man for a toffee.

She was Ram Bharosa's first customer in almost two weeks. He looked suspiciously at the girl. Had she come to taunt him, to flaunt the umbrella in his face? She had placed her coin on the counter. Perhaps it was a bad coin. Ram Bharosa picked it up and bit it; he held it up to the light; he rang it on the ground. It was a good coin. He gave Binya the toffee.

Binya had already left the shop when Ram Bharosa saw the closed umbrella lying on his counter. There it was, the blue umbrella he had always wanted, within his grasp at last! He had only to hide it at the back of his shop, and no one would know that he had it, no one could prove that Binya had left it behind.

He stretched out his trembling, bony hand, and took the umbrella by the handle. He pressed it open. He stood beneath it, in the dark shadows of his shop, where no sun or rain could ever touch it.

'But I'm never in the sun or in the rain,' he said aloud. 'Of what use is an umbrella to me?'

And he hurried outside and ran after Binya.

'Binya, Binya!' he shouted. 'Binya, you've left your umbrella behind!'

He wasn't used to running, but he caught up with her, held out the umbrella, saying, 'You forgot it—the umbrella!'

In that moment it belonged to both of them.

But Binya didn't take the umbrella. She shook her head and said, 'You keep it. I don't need it anymore.'

'But it's such a pretty umbrella!' protested Ram Bharosa. 'It's the best umbrella in the village.'

'I know,' said Binya. 'But an umbrella isn't everything.'

And she left the old man holding the umbrella, and went tripping down the road, and there was nothing between her and the bright blue sky.

VI

Well, now that Ram Bharosa has the blue umbrella—a gift from Binya, as he tells everyone—he is sometimes persuaded to go out into the sun or the rain, and as a result he looks much healthier. Sometimes he uses the umbrella to chase away pigs or goats. It is always left open outside the shop, and anyone who wants to borrow it may do so; and so in a way it has become everyone's umbrella. It is faded and patchy, but it is still the best umbrella in the village.

People are visiting Ram Bharosa's shop again. Whenever Bijju or Binya stop for a cup of tea, he gives them a little extra milk or sugar. They like their tea sweet and milky.

A few nights ago, a bear visited Ram Bharosa's shop. There had been snow on the higher ranges of the Himalaya, and the bear had been finding it difficult to obtain food; so it had come lower down, to see what it could pick up near the village. That night it scrambled on to the tin roof of Ram Bharosa's shop, and made off with a huge pumpkin that had been ripening on the roof. But in climbing off the roof, the bear had lost a claw.

Next morning Ram Bharosa found the claw just outside the door of his shop. He picked it up and put it in his pocket. A bear's claw was a lucky find.

A day later, when he went into the market town, he took the claw with him, and left it with a silversmith, giving the craftsman certain instructions. The silversmith made a locket for the claw, then he gave it a thin silver chain. When Ram Bharosa came again, he paid the silversmith ten rupees for his work.

The days were growing shorter, and Binya had to be home a little earlier every evening. There was a hungry leopard at large, and she couldn't leave the cows out after dark.

She was hurrying past Ram Bharosa's shop when the old man called out to her.

'Binya, spare a minute! I want to show you something.'

Binya stepped into the shop.

'What do you think of it?' asked Ram Bharosa, showing her the silver pendant with the claw.

'It's so beautiful,' said Binya, just touching the claw and the silver chain.

'It's a bear's claw,' said Ram Bharosa. 'That's even luckier than a leopard's claw. Would you like to have it?'

'I have no money,' said Binya.

'That doesn't matter. You gave me the umbrella, I give you the claw! Come, let's see what it looks like on you.'

He placed the pendant on Binya, and indeed it looked very beautiful on her.

Ram Bharosa says he will never forget the smile she gave him when she left the shop.

She was halfway home when she realized she had left the cows behind.

'Neelu, Neelu!' she called. 'Oh, Gori!'

There was a faint tinkle of bells as the cows came slowly down the mountain path.

In the distance she could hear her mother and Bijju calling for her.

She began to sing. They heard her singing, and knew she was safe and near.

She walked home through the darkening glade, singing of the stars, and the trees stood still and listened to her, and the mountains were glad.

WHEN THE MONSOON BREAKS

I was staying at a small hotel in Meerut, in North India. There had been no rain for a month, but the atmosphere was humid, and there were clouds overhead, dark clouds burgeoning with moisture. Thunder blossomed in the air.

The monsoon was going to break that day. I knew it; the birds knew it; the grass knew it. There was the smell of rain in the air. And the grass, the birds and I responded to this odour with the same longing.

A large drop of water hit the windowsill, darkening the thick dust on the woodwork. A faint breeze had sprung up, and again I felt the moisture, closer and warmer.

Then the rain approached like a dark curtain. I could see it moving down the street, heavy and remorseless. It drummed on the corrugated tin roof and swept across the road and over the balcony of my room. I sat there without moving, letting the rain soak my sticky shirt and gritty hair.

Outside, the street rapidly emptied. The crowd disappeared. Then buses, cars and bullock carts plowed through the suddenly rushing water. A group of small boys, gloriously naked, came romping along a side street, which was like a river in spate. A garland of marigolds, swept off the steps of a temple, came floating down the middle of the road. The rain stopped as suddenly as it had begun.

The day was dying, and the breeze remained cool and moist. In the brief twilight that followed, I was witness to the great yearly flight of insects into the cool, brief freedom of the night.

Termites and white ants, which had been sleeping through

the hot season, emerged from their lairs. Out of every hole and crack, and from under the roots of trees, huge winged ants emerged, at first fluttering about heavily on this, the first and last flight of their lives. There was only one direction in which they could fly—towards the light—towards the street lights and the bright neon tubelight above my balcony.

The light above my balcony attracted a massive, quivering swarm of clumsy termites, giving the impression of one thick, slowly revolving mass. A frog had found its way through the bathroom and came hopping across the balcony to pause beneath the light. All he had to do was gobble, as insects fell around him.

This was the hour of the geckos, the wall lizards. They had their reward for weeks of patient waiting. Plying their sticky pink tongues, they devoured insects as swiftly and methodically as children devour popcorn. For hours they crammed their stomachs, knowing that such a feast would not come their way again. Throughout the entire hot season the insect world had prepared for this flight out of darkness into light, and the phenomenon would not happen again for another year.

In hot up-country towns in India, it is good to have the first monsoon showers arrive at night, while you are sleeping on the veranda. You wake up to the scent of wet earth and fallen neem leaves, and find that a hot and stuffy bungalow has been convened into a cool, damp place.

The swish of the banana fronds and the drumming of the rain on broad-leaved sal trees will soothe any brow.

During the rains, the frogs have a perfect country music festival. There are two sets of them, it seems, and they sing antiphonal chants all evening, each group letting the other take its turn in the fairest manner. No one sees or hears them during the hot weather, but the moment the monsoon breaks, they swarm all over the place.

When night comes on, great moths fly past, and beetles of all shapes and sizes come whirring in at the open windows. The fireflies also light up their lamps, flashing messages to each other through the mango groves. Some nocturnal insects thrive mainly at the expense of humans, and sometimes one wakes up to find thirty or forty mosquitoes looking through the netting in a hungry manner. If you are sleeping out, you'll need that mosquito-netting.

The road outside is lined with line *babul* trees, now covered with powdery little halls of yellow blossom, filling the air with a faint scent. After the first showers, there is a great deal of water about, and for many miles the trees are standing in it. The common sights along an up-country road are often picturesque—the wide plains with great herds of smoke-coloured, delicate-limbed cattle being driven slowly home for the night, accompanied by troops of ungainly buffaloes, and flocks of goats and black long-tailed sheep. Then you come to a pond, where the buffaloes are indulging in a wallow, no part of them visible but the tips of their noses.

Within a few days of the first rain, the air is full of dragonflies, crossing and recrossing, poised motionless for a moment, then darting away with that mingled grace and power that is unmatched among insects. Dragonflies are the swallows of the insect world; their prey is the mosquitoes, the gnats, the midges and the flies. These swarms, therefore, tell us that the moistened surface of the ground, with its mouldering leaves and sodden grass, has become one vast incubator teeming with every form of ephemeral life.

After the monotony of a fierce sun and a dusty landscape quartering in the dim distance, one welcomes these days of mild light, green earth and purple hills coming near in the clear and transparent air.

And later on, when the monsoon begins to break up and the hills are dappled with light and shade, dark islands of clouds moving across the bright green sea, the effect on one's spirit is strangely exhilarating. For in India, the true spring, the beginning of things, the birthday of nature, is not in March but in June.

BUS STOP, PIPALNAGAR

I

M y balcony was my window to the world.
The room itself had only one window, a square hole in
the wall crossed by two iron bars. The view from it was rather
restricted. If I craned my neck sideways, and put my nose to
the bars, I could see the end of the building. Below was a
narrow courtyard where children played. Across the courtyard,
level with my room, were three separate windows belonging
to three separate rooms, each window barred in the same way,
with iron bars. During the day it was difficult to see into these
rooms. The harsh, cruel sunlight filled the courtyard, making
the windows patches of darkness.

My room was very small. I had paced about in it so often
that I knew its exact measurements. My foot, from heel to toe,
was eleven inches long. That made my room just over fifteen
feet in length; for, when I measured the last foot, my toes
turned up against the wall. It wasn't more than eight feet broad,
which meant that two people was the most it could comfortably
accommodate. I was the only tenant but at times I had put up
at least three friends—two on the floor, two on the bed. The
plaster had been peeling off the walls and in addition the greasy
stains and patches were difficult to hide, though I covered the
worst ones with pictures cut out from magazines—Waheeda
Rehman, the Indian actress, successfully blotted out one big
patch and a recent Mr Universe displayed his muscles from
the opposite wall. The biggest stain was all but concealed by a

calendar that showed Ganesh, the elephant-headed god, whose blessings were vital to all good beginnings.

My belongings were few. A shelf on the wall supported an untidy pile of paperbacks, and a small table in one corner of the room supported the solid weight of my rejected manuscripts and an ancient typewriter that I had obtained on hire.

I was eighteen years old and a writer.

Such a combination would be disastrous enough anywhere, but in India it was doubly so; for there were not many papers to write for and payments were small. In addition, I was very inexperienced and though what I wrote came from the heart, only a fraction touched the hearts of editors. Nevertheless, I persevered and was able to earn about a hundred rupees a month, barely enough to keep body, soul and typewriter together. There wasn't much else I could do. Without that passport to a job—a university degree—I had no alternative but to accept the classification of 'self-employed'—which was impressive as it included doctors, lawyers, property dealers and grain merchants, most of whom earned well over a thousand rupees a month.

'Haven't you realized that India is bursting with young people trying to pass exams?' asked a journalist friend. 'It's a desperate matter, this race for academic qualifications. Everyone wants to pass his exam the easy way, without reading too many books or attending more than half-a-dozen lectures. That's where a smart fellow like you comes in! Why would students wade through five volumes of political history when they can buy a few model answer papers at any bookstall? They are helpful, these guess papers. You can write them quickly and flood the market. They'll sell like hot cakes!'

'Who eats hot cakes here?'

'Well, then, hot chapattis.'

'I'll think about it,' I said; but the idea repelled me. If

I was going to misguide students, I would rather do it by writing second-rate detective stories than by providing them with readymade answer papers. Besides, I thought it would bore me.

II

The string of the cot needed tightening. The dip in the middle of the bed was so bad that I woke up in the morning with a stiff back. But I was hopeless at tightening bed-strings and would have to wait until one of the boys from the tea shop paid me a visit. I was too tall for the cot, anyway, and if my feet didn't stick out at one end, my head lolled over the other.

Under the cot was my tin trunk. Apart from my clothes, it contained notebooks, diaries, photographs, scrapbooks, and other odds and ends that form a part of a writer's existence.

I did not live entirely alone. During cold or rainy weather, the boys from the tea shop, who normally slept on the pavement, crowded into the room. Apart from them, there were lizards on the walls and ceilings—friends these—and a large rat—definitely an enemy—who got in and out of the window and who sometimes carried away manuscripts and clothing.

June nights were the most uncomfortable. Mosquitoes emerged from all the ditches, gullies and ponds, to swarm over Pipalnagar. Bugs, finding it uncomfortable inside the woodwork of the cot, scrambled out at night and found their way under the sheet. The lizards wandered listlessly over the walls, impatient for the monsoon rains, when they would be able to feast off thousands of insects.

Everyone in Pipalnagar was waiting for the cool, quenching relief of the monsoon.

III

I woke every morning at five as soon as the first bus moved out of the shed, situated only twenty or thirty yards down the road. I dressed, went down to the tea shop for a glass of hot tea and some buttered toast, and then visited Deep Chand the barber in his shop.

At eighteen, I shaved about three times a week. Sometimes I shaved myself. But often, when I felt lazy, Deep Chand shaved me, at the special concessional rate of two annas.

'Give my head a good massage, Deep Chand,' I said. 'My brain is not functioning these days. In my latest story there are three murders, but it is boring just the same.'

'You must write a good book,' said Deep Chand, beginning the ritual of the head massage, his fingers squeezing my temples and tugging at my hair-roots. 'Then you can make some money and clear out of Pipalnagar. Delhi is the place to go! Why, I know a man who arrived in Delhi in 1947 with nothing but the clothes he wore and a few rupees. He began by selling thirsty travellers glasses of cold water at the railway station, then he opened a small tea shop; now he has two big restaurants and lives in a house as large as the prime minister's!'

Nobody intended to live in Pipalnagar forever. Delhi was the city most aspired to but as it was 200 miles away, few could afford to travel there.

Deep Chand would have shifted his trade to another town if he had had the capital. In Pipalnagar his main customers were small shopkeepers, factory workers and labourers from the railway station. 'Here I can charge only six annas for a haircut,' he lamented. 'In Delhi I could charge a rupee.'

IV

I was walking in the wheat fields beyond the railway tracks when I noticed a boy lying across the footpath, his head and shoulders hidden by wheat plants. I walked faster, and when I came near I saw that the boy's legs were twitching. He seemed to be having some kind of fit. The boy's face was white, his legs kept moving and his hands fluttered restlessly among the wheat stalks.

'What's the matter?' I said, kneeling down beside him but he was still unconscious.

I ran down the path to a Persian well, and dipping the end of my shirt in a shallow trough of water, soaked it well before returning to the boy. As I sponged his face, the twitching ceased, and though he still breathed heavily, his face was calm and his hands still. He opened his eyes and stared at me, but he didn't really see me.

'You have bitten your tongue,' I said, wiping a little blood from the corner of his mouth. 'Don't worry. I'll stay here with you until you are all right.'

The boy raised himself and, resting his chin on his knees, he passed his arms around his drawn-up legs.

'I'm all right now,' he said.

'What happened?' I asked, sitting down beside him.

'Oh, it is nothing, it often happens. I don't know why. I cannot control it.'

'Have you been to a doctor?'

'Yes, when the fits first started, I went to the hospital. They gave me some pills that I had to take every day. But the pills made me so tired and sleepy that I couldn't work properly. So I stopped taking them. Now this happens once or twice a week. What does it matter? I'm all right when it's over and I do not feel anything when it happens.'

He got to his feet, dusting his clothes and smiling at me. He was a slim boy, long-limbed and bony. There was a little fluff on his cheeks and the promise of a moustache. He told me his name was Suraj, that he went to a night school in the city, and that he hoped to finish his high school exams in a few months' time. He was studying hard, he said, and if he passed he hoped to get a scholarship to a good college. If he failed, there was only the prospect of continuing in Pipalnagar.

I noticed a small tray of merchandise lying on the ground. It contained combs and buttons and little bottles of perfume. The tray was made to hang at Suraj's waist, supported by straps that went around his shoulders. All day he walked about Pipalnagar, sometimes covering ten or fifteen miles, selling odds and ends to people in their houses. He averaged about two rupees a day, which was enough for his food and other necessities; he managed to save about ten rupees a month for his school fees. He ate irregularly at little tea shops, at the stall near the bus stop, under the shady jamun and mango trees. When the jamun fruit was ripe, he would sit on a tree, sucking the sour fruit until his lips were stained purple. There was a small, nagging fear that he might get a fit while sitting on the tree and fall off, but the temptation to eat jamun was greater than his fear.

All this he told me while we walked through the fields towards the bazaar.

'Where do you live?' I asked. 'I'll walk home with you.'

'I don't live anywhere,' said Suraj. 'My home is not in Pipalnagar. Sometimes I sleep at the temple or at the railway station. In the summer months I sleep on the grass of the municipal park.'

'Well, wherever it is you stay, let me come with you.'

We walked together into the town, and parted near the bus stop. I returned to my room, and tried to do some writing while Suraj went to the bazaar to try selling his wares. We had agreed to meet each other again. I realized that Suraj was an epileptic, but there was nothing unusual about him being an orphan and a refugee. I liked his positive attitude to life. Most people in Pipalnagar were resigned to their circumstances but he was ambitious. I also liked his gentleness, his quiet voice, and the smile that flickered across his face regardless of whether he was sad or happy.

V

The temperature had touched forty-three degrees Celsius, and the small streets of Pipalnagar were empty. To walk barefoot on the scorching pavements was possible only for labourers, whose feet had developed several hard layers of protective skin; and now even these hardy men lay stretched out in the shade provided by trees and buildings.

I hadn't written anything in two weeks, and though one or two small payments were due from a Delhi newspaper, I could think of no substantial amount that was likely to come my way in the near future. I decided that I would dash off a couple of articles that same night, and post them the following morning.

Having made this comforting decision, I lay down on the floor in preference to the cot. I liked the touch of things; the touch of a cool floor on a hot day, the touch of earth—soft, grassy grass was good, especially dew-drenched grass. Wet earth was soft, sensuous, as was splashing through puddles and streams.

I slept, and dreamt of a cool, clear stream in a forest glade, where I bathed in gay abandon. A little further downstream was another bather. I hailed him, expecting to see Suraj, but when the bather turned I found that it was my landlord's pot-bellied rent collector, holding an accounts ledger in his hands. This woke me up, and for the remainder of the day I worked feverishly at my articles.

Next morning, when I opened the door, I found Suraj asleep at the top of the steps. His tray lay at the bottom of the steps. He woke up as soon as I touched his shoulder.

'Have you been sleeping here all night?' I asked. 'Why didn't you come in?'

'It was very late,' said Suraj. 'I didn't want to disturb you.'

'Someone could have stolen your things while you were asleep.'

'Oh, I sleep quite lightly. Besides I have nothing of great value. But I came here to ask you a favour.'

'You need money?'

He laughed. 'Do all your friends mean money when they ask for favours? No, I want you to take your meal with me tonight.'

'But where? You have no place of your own and it would be too expensive in a restaurant.'

'In your room,' said Suraj. 'I shall bring the meat and vegetables and cook them here. Do you have a cooker?'

'I think so,' I said, scratching my head in some perplexity. 'I will have to look for it.'

Suraj brought a chicken for dinner—a luxury, one to be indulged in only two or three times a year. He had bought the bird for seven rupees, which was cheap. We spiced it and roasted it on a spit.

'I wish we could do this more often,' I said, as I dug my teeth into the soft flesh of a second chicken leg.

'We could do it at least once a month if we worked hard,' said Suraj.

'You know how to work. You work from morning to evening and then you work again.'

'But you are a writer. That is different. You have to wait for the right moment.'

I laughed. 'Moods and moments are for geniuses. No, it's really a matter of working hard, and I'm just plain lazy, to tell you the truth.'

'Perhaps you are writing the wrong things.'

'Perhaps, I wish I could do something else. Even if I repaired bicycle tyres, I'd make more money!'

'Then why don't you repair bicycle tyres?'

'Oh, I would rather be a bad writer than a good repairer of cycle tyres.' I brightened up, 'I could go into business, though. Do you know I once owned a vegetable stall?'

'Wonderful! When was that?'

'A couple of months ago. But it failed after two days.'

'Then you are not good at business. Let us think of something else.'

'I can tell fortunes with cards.'

'There are already too many fortune tellers in Pipalnagar.'

'Then we won't talk of fortunes. And you must sleep here tonight. It is better than sleeping on the roadside.'

VI

At noon when the shadows shifted and crossed the road, a band of children rushed down the empty street, shouting and waving their satchels. They had been at their desks from early morning, and now, despite the hot sun, they would have their fling while their elders slept on string charpoys beneath leafy neem trees.

On the soft sand near the riverbed, boys wrestled or played leapfrog. At alley corners, where tall buildings shaded narrow passages, the favourite game was *gulli-danda*. The gulli—a small piece of wood, about four inches long sharpened to a point at each end—is struck with the danda—a short, stout stick. A player is allowed three hits, and his score is the distance, in danda lengths, of his hits of the gulli. Boys who were experts at the game sent the gulli flying far down the road—sometimes into a shop or through a windowpane, which resulted in confusion, loud invective, and a dash for cover.

A game for both children and young men was kabaddi. This is a game that calls for good breath control and much agility. It is also known in different parts of India as hootoo-too, kho-kho and atya patya. Ramu, Deep Chand's younger brother, excelled at this game. He was the Pipalnagar kabaddi champion.

The game is played by two teams, consisting of eight or nine members each, who face each other across a dividing line. Each side in turn sends out one of its players into the opponent's area. This person has to keep on saying 'kabaddi, kabaddi' very fast and without taking a second breath. If he returns to his side after touching an opponent, that opponent is 'dead' and out of the game. If, however, he is caught and cannot struggle back to his side while still holding his breath, he is 'dead'.

Ramu, who was also a good wrestler, knew all the kabaddi holds, and was particularly good at capturing opponents. He had vitality and confidence, rare things in Pipalnagar. He wanted to go into the army after finishing school; a happy choice, I thought.

VII

Suraj did not know if his parents were dead or alive. He had literally lost them when he was six. His father had been a farmer, a dark, unfathomable man who spoke little, thought perhaps even less and was vaguely aware he had a son—a weak boy given to introspection and dawdling at the riverbank when he should have been helping in the fields.

Suraj's mother had been a subdued, silent woman, frail and consumptive. Her husband seemed to expect that she would not live long, but Suraj did not know if she was living or dead. He had lost his parents at Amritsar railway station in the days of Partition, when trains coming across the border from Pakistan disgorged themselves of thousands of refugees or pulled into the station half-empty, drenched with blood and littered with corpses.

Suraj and his parents had been lucky to escape one of these massacres. Had they travelled on an earlier train (which they had tried desperately to catch), they might have been killed. Suraj was clinging to his mother's sari while she tried to keep up with her husband who was elbowing his way through the frightened, bewildered throng of refugees. Suraj collided with a burly Sikh and lost his grip on the sari. The Sikh had a long curved sword at his waist, and Suraj stared up at him in awe and fascination—at the man's long hair, which had fallen loose, at his wild black beard, and at the bloodstains on his white shirt. The Sikh pushed him aside and when Suraj looked around for his mother, she was not to be seen. She was hidden from him by a mass of restless bodies, all pushing in different directions. He could hear her calling his name and he tried to force his way through the crowd in the direction of her voice, but he was carried on the other way.

At night, when the platform emptied, he was still searching for his mother. Eventually, the police came and took him away. They looked for his parents but without success, and finally they sent him to a home for orphans. Many children lost their parents at about the same time.

Suraj stayed at the orphanage for two years and when he was eight, and felt himself a man, he ran away. He worked for some time as a helper in a tea shop; but when he started having epileptic fits the shopkeeper asked him to leave, and the boy found himself on the streets, begging for a living. He begged for a year, moving from one town to the next and finally ended up in Pipalnagar. By then he was twelve and really too old to beg, but he had saved some money, and with it he bought a small stock of combs, buttons, cheap perfumes and bangles, and, converting himself into a mobile shop, went from door to door selling his wares.

Pipalnagar is a small town and there was no house that Suraj hadn't visited. Everyone knew him; some had offered him food and drink; and the children liked him because he often played on a small flute when he went on his rounds.

VIII

Suraj came to see me quite often and, when he stayed late, he slept in my room, curling up on the floor and sleeping fitfully. He would always leave early in the morning before I could get him anything to eat.

'Should I go to Delhi, Suraj?' I asked him one evening.

'Why not? In Delhi, there are many ways of making money.'

'And spending it too. Why don't you come with me?'

'After my exams, perhaps. Not now.'

'Well, I can wait. I don't want to live alone in a big city.'

'In the meantime, write your book.'

'All right, I will try.'

We decided we could try to save a little money from Suraj's earnings and my own occasional payments from newspapers and magazines. Even if we were to give Delhi only a few days' trial, we would need money to live on. We managed to put away twenty rupees one week, but withdrew it the next when a friend, Pitamber, asked for a loan to repair his cycle rickshaw. He returned the money in three instalments but we could not save any of it. Pitamber and Deep Chand also had plans of going to Delhi. Pitamber wanted to own his own cycle rickshaw; Deep Chand dreamt of a swanky barber shop in the capital.

One day Suraj and I hired bicycles and rode out of Pipalnagar. It was a hot, sunny morning and we were perspiring after we had gone two miles, but a fresh wind sprang up suddenly, and we could smell the rain in the air though there were no clouds to be seen.

'Let us go where there are no people at all,' said Suraj. 'I am a little tired of people. I see too many of them all day.'

We got down from our cycles and, pushing them off the road, took a path through a paddy field and then one through a field of young maize, and in the distance we saw a tree, a crooked tree, growing beside a well. I do not even today know the name of that tree. I had never seen its kind before. It had a crooked trunk, crooked branches and it was clothed in thick, broad, crooked leaves, like the leaves on which food is served in bazaars.

In the trunk of the tree was a large hole and when I sat my cycle down with a crash, two green parrots flew out of the hole, and went dipping and swerving across the fields.

There was grass around the well, cropped short by grazing cattle, so we sat in the shade of the crooked tree and Suraj untied the red cloth in which we had brought food. We ate our bread and vegetable curry; meanwhile the parrots returned to the tree.

'Let us come here every week,' said Suraj, stretching himself out on the grass. It was a drowsy day, the air was humid and he soon fell asleep. I was aware of different sensations. I heard a cricket singing in the tree; the cooing of pigeons that lived in the walls of the old well; the soft breathing of Suraj; a rustling in the leaves of the tree; the distant drone of the bees. I smelt the grass and the old bricks around the well, and the promise of rain.

When I opened my eyes, I saw dark clouds on the horizon. Suraj was still sleeping with his arms thrown across his face to keep the glare out of his eyes. As I was thirsty, I went to the well and, putting my shoulders to it, turned the wheel very slowly, walking around the well four times, while cool clean water gushed out over the stones and along the channel to the fields. I drank from one of the trays, and the water tasted sweet; the deeper the wells, the sweeter the water. Suraj was sitting up now, looking at the sky.

'It's going to rain,' he said.

We pushed our cycles back to the main road and began riding homewards. We were a mile out of Pipalnagar when it began to rain. A lashing wind swept the rain across our faces, but we exulted in it and sang at the top of our voices until we reached the bus stop. Leaving the cycles at the hire shop, we ran up the rickety, swaying steps to my room.

In the evening, as the bazaar was lighting up, the rain stopped. We went to sleep quite early, but at midnight I was woken by the moon shining full on my face—a full moon, shedding its light all over Pipalnagar, peeping and prying into every home, washing the empty streets, silvering the corrugated tin roofs.

IX

The lizards hung listlessly on the walls and ceilings, waiting for the monsoon rains, which bring out all the insects from their cracks and crannies.

One day, clouds loomed upon the horizon, growing rapidly into enormous towers. A faint breeze sprang up, bringing with it the first of the monsoon raindrops. This was the moment everyone was waiting for. People ran out of their houses to take in the fresh breeze and the scent of those first few raindrops on the parched, dusty earth. Underground, in their cracks, the insects were moving. Termites and white ants, which had been sleeping through the hot season, emerged from their lairs.

And then, on the second or third night of the monsoon, came the great yearly flight of insects into the cool, brief freedom of the night. Out of every crack, from under the roots of trees, huge winged ants emerged, at first fluttering about heavily, on the first and last flight of their lives. At night there was only one direction in which they could fly—towards the light; towards the electric bulbs and smoky kerosene lamps throughout Pipalnagar. The street lamp opposite the bus stop, beneath my room, attracted a massive, quivering swarm of clumsy termites, which gave the impression of one thick, slowly-revolving body.

This was the hour of the lizards. Now they had their reward for those days of patient waiting. Plying their sticky pink tongues, they devoured the insects as fast as they came. For hours, they crammed their stomachs, knowing that such a feast would not be theirs again for another year. How wasteful nature is, I thought. Through the whole hot season the insect world prepares for the flight out of the darkness into light and not one of them survives its freedom.

Suraj and I walked barefooted over the cool, wet pavements, across the railway lines and the riverbed, until we were not far from the crooked tree. Dotting the landscape were old abandoned brick kilns. When it rained heavily, the hollows made by the kilns filled up with water. Suraj and I found a small tank where we could bathe and swim. On a mound in the middle of the tank stood a ruined hut, formerly inhabited by a watchman at the kiln. We swam and then wrestled on the young green grass. Though I was heavier than Suraj and my chest as sound as a new drum, he had a lot of power in his long, wiry arms and legs, and he pinioned me about the waist with his bony knees. And then suddenly, as I strained to press his back to the ground, I felt his body go tense. He stiffened, his thigh jerked against me and his legs began to twitch. I knew that a fit was coming on, but I was unable to get out of his grip. He held me more tightly as the fit took possession of him.

When I noticed his mouth working, I thrust the palm of my hand in, sideways, to prevent him from biting his tongue. But so violent was the convulsion that his teeth bit into my flesh. I shouted with pain and tried to pull my hand away, but he was unconscious and his jaw was set. I closed my eyes and counted slowly up to seven and then I felt his muscles relax and I was able to take my hand away. It was bleeding a little but I bound it with a handkerchief before Suraj fully regained consciousness.

He didn't say much as we walked back to town. He looked depressed and weak, but I knew it wouldn't take long for him to recover his usual good spirits. He did not notice that I kept my hand out of sight and only after he had returned from classes that night did he notice the bandage and asked what happened.

X

'Do you want to make some money?' asked Pitamber, bursting into the room like a festive cracker.

'I do,' I said.

'What do we have to do for it?' asked Suraj, striking a cautious note.

'Oh nothing, carry a banner and walk in front of a procession.'

'Why?'

'Don't ask me. Some political stunt.'

'Which party?'

'I don't know. Who cares? All I know is that they are paying two rupees a day to anyone who'll carry a flag or banner.'

'We don't need two rupees that badly,' I said. 'And you can make more than that in a day with your rickshaw.'

'True, but they're paying me *five*. They're fixing a loudspeaker to my rickshaw, and one of the party's men will sit in it and make speeches as we go along. Come on, it will be fun.'

'No banners for us,' I said. 'But we may come along and watch.'

And we did watch, when, later that morning, the procession passed along our street. It was a ragged procession of about a hundred people, shouting slogans. Some of them were children, and some of them were men who did not know what it was all about, but all joined in the slogan-shouting.

We didn't know much about it, either. Because, though the

man in Pitamber's rickshaw was loud and eloquent, his loudspeaker was defective, with the result that his words were punctuated with squeaks and an eerie whining sound. Pitamber looked up and saw us standing on the balcony and gave us a wave and a wide grin. We decided to follow the procession at a discreet distance. It was a protest march against something or other; we never did manage to find out the details. The destination was the municipal office, and by the time we got there the crowd had increased to two or three hundred people. Some rowdies had now joined in, and things began to get out of hand. The man in the rickshaw continued his speech; another man standing on a wall was making a speech; and someone from the municipal office was confronting the crowd and making a speech of his own.

A stone was thrown, then another. From a sprinkling of stones, it soon became a shower of stones; and then some police constables, who had been standing by watching the fun, were ordered into action. They ran at the crowd where it was thinnest, brandishing stout sticks.

We were caught in the stampede that followed. A stone—flung no doubt at a policeman—was badly aimed and struck me on the shoulder. Suraj pulled me down a side street. Looking back, we saw Pitamber's cycle rickshaw lying on its side in the middle of the road, but there was no sign of Pitamber.

Later, he turned up in my room, with a cut over his left eyebrow that was bleeding freely. Suraj washed the cut, and I poured iodine over it—Pitamber did not flinch—and covered it with sticking plaster. The cut was quite deep and should have had stitches, but Pitamber was superstitious about hospitals, saying he knew very few people to come out of them alive. He was of course thinking about the Pipalnagar hospital.

So he acquired a scar on his forehead. It went rather well with his demonic good looks.

XI

'Thank God for the monsoon,' said Suraj. 'We won't have any more demonstrations on the roads until the weather improves!'

And, until the rain stopped, Pipalnagar was fresh and clean and alive. The children ran naked out of their houses and romped through the streets. The gutters overflowed, and the road became a mountain stream, coursing merrily towards the bus stop.

At the bus stop there was confusion. Newly arrived passengers, surrounded on all sides by a sea of mud and rainwater, were met by scores of tongas and cycle rickshaws, each jostling the other trying to cater to the passengers. As a result, only half found conveyances, while the other half found themselves knee-deep in Pipalnagar mud.

Pipalnagar mud has a quality all its own—and it is not easily removed or forgotten. Only buffaloes love it because it is soft and squelchy. Two parts of it are thick, sticky clay that seems to come alive at the slightest touch, clinging tenaciously to human flesh. Feet sink into it and have to be wrenched out. Fingers become webbed. Get it into your hair, and there is nothing you can do except go to Deep Chand and have your head shaved.

London has its fog, Paris its sewers, Pipalnagar its mud. Pitamber, of course, succeeded in getting as his passenger the most attractive girl to step off the bus, and showed her his skill and daring by taking her to her destination by the longest and roughest road.

The rain swirled over the trees and roofs of the town, and the parched earth soaked it up, giving out a fresh smell that came only once a year, the fragrance of quenched earth, that loveliest of all smells.

In my room I was battling against the elements, for the door would not close, and the rain swept into the room and soaked my cot. When finally I succeeded in closing the door, I discovered that the roof was leaking and the water was trickling down the walls, running through the dusty design I had made with my feet. I placed tins and mugs in strategic positions and, satisfied that everything was now under control, sat on the cot to watch the rooftops through my windows.

There was a loud banging on the door. It flew open, and there was Suraj standing on the threshold, drenched. Coming in, he began to dry himself while I made desperate efforts to close the door again.

'Let's make some tea,' he said.

Glasses of hot, sweet milky tea on a rainy day...it was enough to make me feel fresh and full of optimism. We sat on the cot, enjoying the brew.

'One day, I'll write a book,' I said. 'Not just a thriller, but a real book, about real people. Perhaps about you and me and Pipalnagar. And then we'll be famous and our troubles will be over and new troubles will begin. I don't mind problems as long as they are new. While you're studying, I'll write my book. I'll start tonight. It is an auspicious time, the first night of the monsoon.'

A tree must have fallen across the wires somewhere, because the lights would not come on. So I lit a small oil lamp, and while it spluttered in the steamy darkness Suraj opened his book and, with one hand on the book, the other playing with his toe—this helped him to concentrate!—he began to study. I took the inkpot down from the shelf, and, finding it empty, added a little rainwater to it from one of the mugs. I sat down beside Suraj and began to write, but the pen was no good and made blotches all over the paper. And, although I was full of writing just then, I didn't really know what I wanted to say.

So I went out and began pacing up and down the road.

There I found Pitamber, a little drunk, very merry, and prancing about in the middle of the road.

'What are you dancing for?' I asked.

'I'm happy, so I'm dancing,' said Pitamber.

'And why are you happy?' I asked.

'Because I'm dancing,' he said.

The rain stopped and the neem trees gave out a strong, sweet smell.

XII

Flowers in Pipalnagar—did they exist? As a child I knew a garden in Lucknow where there were beds of phlox and petunias and another garden where only roses grew. In the fields around Pipalnagar was thorn apple—a yellow buttercup nestling among thorn leaves. But in Pipalnagar Bazaar there were no flowers except one—a marigold growing out of a crack on my balcony. I had removed the plaster from the base of the plant, and filled in a little earth that I watered every morning. The plant was healthy, and sometimes it produced a small orange marigold.

Sometimes Suraj plucked a flower and kept it in his tray, among the combs, buttons and scent bottles. Sometimes he gave the flower to a passing child, once to a small boy who immediately tore it to shreds. Suraj was back on his rounds, as his exams were over.

Whenever he was tired of going from house to house, Suraj would sit beneath a shady banyan or peepul tree, put his tray aside, and take out his flute. The haunting notes travelled down the road in the afternoon stillness, drawing children to him. They would sit beside him and be very quiet when he played, because there was something melancholic and appealing about the tune. Suraj sometimes made flutes out of pieces of bamboo, but he never sold them. He would give them to the children he liked. He would sell almost anything, but not flutes.

Suraj sometimes played the flute at night, when he lay awake, unable to sleep; but even though I slept, I could hear the music in my dreams. Sometimes he took his flute with him to the crooked tree and played for the benefit of the birds. The parrots made harsh noises in response and flew away. Once, when Suraj was playing his flute to a small group of children, he had a fit. The flute fell from his hands. And he began to roll about in the dust on the roadside. The children became frightened and ran away, but they did not stay away for long. The next time they heard the flute, they came to listen as usual.

XIII

It was Lord Krishna's birthday, and the rain came down as heavily as it is said to have done on the day he was born. Krishna is the best beloved of all the gods. Young mothers laugh or weep as they read or hear the pranks of his boyhood; young men pray to be as tall and as strong as Krishna was when he killed King Kamsa's elephant and wrestlers; young girls dream of a lover as daring as Krishna to carry them off in a war chariot; grown men envy the wisdom and statesmanship with which he managed the affairs of his kingdom.

The rain came so unexpectedly that it took everyone by surprise. In seconds, people were drenched, and within minutes, the streets were flooded. The temple tank overflowed, the railway lines disappeared, and the old wall near the bus stop shivered and silently fell—the sound of its collapse drowned in the downpour. A naked young man with a dancing bear cavorted in the middle of the vegetable market. Pitamber's rickshaw churned through the floodwater while he sang lustily as he worked.

Wading through knee-deep water down the road, I saw the roadside vendors salvaging whatever they could. Plastic toys, cabbages and utensils floated away and were seized by urchins. The water had risen to the level of the shop fronts and the floors were awash. Deep Chand and Ramu, with the help of a customer, were using buckets to bail the water out of their shop. The rain stopped as suddenly as it had begun and the sun came out. The water began to find an outlet, flooding other low-lying areas, and a paper boat came sailing between my legs.

Next morning, the morning on which the result of Suraj's examinations was due, I rose early—the first time I ever got up before Suraj—and went down to the news agency. A small crowd of students had gathered at the bus stop, joking with each other and hiding their nervousness with a show of indifference. There were not many passengers on the first bus, and there was a mad grab for newspapers as the bundle landed with a thud on the pavement. Within half-an-hour, the newsboy had sold all his copies. It was the best day of the year for him.

I went through the columns relating to Pipalnagar, but I couldn't find Suraj's roll number on the list of successful candidates. I had the number on a slip of paper, and I looked at it again to make sure I had compared it correctly with the others; then I went through the newspaper once more. When I returned to the room, Suraj was sitting on the doorstep. I didn't have to tell him he had failed—he knew by the look on my face. I sat down beside him, and we said nothing for some time.

'Never mind,' Suraj said eventually. 'I will pass next time.'

I realized I was more depressed than he was and that he was trying to console me.

'If only you'd had more time,' I said.

'I have a year. And you will have time to finish your book, and then we can go away together. Another year of Pipalnagar won't be so bad. As long as I have your friendship almost everything can be tolerated.'

He stood up, the tray hanging from his shoulders. 'Is there anything you'd like to buy?'

XIV

Another year of Pipalnagar! But it was not to be. A short time later, I received a letter from the editor of a newspaper, calling me to Delhi for an interview. My friends insisted that I should go. Such an opportunity would not come again.

But I needed a shirt. The few I possessed were either frayed at the collar or torn at the shoulders. I hadn't been able to afford a new shirt for over a year, and I couldn't afford one now. Struggling writers weren't expected to dress well, but I felt in order to get the job I would need both a haircut and a clean shirt.

Where was I to go to get a shirt? Suraj generally wore an old red-striped T-shirt; he washed it every second evening, and by morning it was dry and ready to wear again; but it was tight even on him. He did not have another. Besides, I needed something white, something respectable!

I went to Deep Chand, who had a collection of shirts. He was only too glad to lend me one. But they were all brightly coloured—pinks, purples and magentas... No editor was going to be impressed by a young writer in a pink shirt. They looked fine on Deep Chand, but he had no need to look respectable.

Finally, Pitamber came to my rescue. He didn't bother with shirts himself, except in winter, but he was able to borrow a clean white shirt from a guard at the jail, who'd got it from the relative of a convict in exchange for certain favours.

'This shirt will make you look respectable,' said Pitamber. 'To be respectable—what an adventure!'

XV

Freedom. The moment the bus was out of Pipalnagar, and the fields opened out on all sides, I knew that I was free, that I had always been free. Only my own weakness, hesitation, and the habits that had grown around me had held me back. All I had to do was sit in a bus and go somewhere.

I sat near the open window of the bus and let the cool breeze from the fields play against my face. Herons and snipe waded among the lotus roots in flat green ponds. Blue jays swooped around telegraph poles. Children jumped naked into the canals that wound through the fields. Because I was happy, it seemed to me that everyone else was happy—the driver, the conductor, the passengers, the farmers in the fields and those driving bullock carts. When two women behind me started quarrelling over their seats, I helped to placate them. Then I took a small girl on my knee and pointed out camels, buffaloes, vultures and pariah dogs.

Six hours later, the bus crossed the bridge over the swollen Yamuna River, passed under the walls of the great Red Fort built by a Mughal emperor, and entered the old city of Delhi. I found it strange to be in a city again, after several years in Pipalnagar. It was a little frightening too. I felt like a stranger. No one was interested in me.

In Pipalnagar, people wanted to know each other, or at least to know about one another. In Delhi, no one cared who you were or where you came from, like big cities almost everywhere. It was prosperous but without a heart.

After a day and a night of loneliness, I found myself wishing that Suraj had accompanied me; wishing that I was back in Pipalnagar. But when the job was offered to me—at a starting salary of three hundred rupees per month, a princely sum compared to what I had been making on my own—I did not have the courage to refuse it. After accepting the job—which was to commence in a week's time—I spent the day wandering through the bazaars, down the wide, shady roads of the capital, resting under the jamun trees, and thinking all the time what I would do in the months to come.

I slept at the railway waiting room and all night long I heard the shunting and whistling of engines, which conjured up visions of places with sweet names like Kumbakonam, Krishnagiri, Polonnarurawa. I dreamt of palm-fringed beaches and inland lagoons; of the echoing chambers of deserted cities, red sandstone and white marble; of temples in the sun; and elephants crossing wide, slow-moving rivers...

XVI

Pitamber was on the platform when the train steamed into the Pipalnagar station in the early hours of a damp September morning. I waved to him from the carriage window, and shouted that everything had gone well.

But everything was not well here. When I got off the train, Pitamber told me that Suraj had been ill—that he'd had a fit on a lonely stretch of road the previous afternoon and had lain in the sun for over an hour. Pitamber had found him, suffering from heatstroke, and brought him home. When I saw him, he was sitting up on the string bed drinking hot tea. He looked pale and weak, but his smile was reassuring.

'Don't worry,' he said. 'I will be all right.'

'He was bad last night,' said Pitamber. 'He had a fever and kept talking, as in a dream. But what he says is true—he is better this morning.'

'Thanks to Pitamber,' said Suraj. 'It is good to have friends.'

'Come with me to Delhi, Suraj,' I said. 'I have got a job

now. You can live with me and attend a school regularly.'

'It is good for friends to help each other,' said Suraj, 'but only after I have passed my exam will I join you in Delhi. I made myself this promise. Poor Pipalnagar—nobody wants to stay here. Will you be sorry to leave?'

'Yes, I will be sorry. A part of me will still be here.'

XVII

Deep Chand was happy to know that I was leaving. 'I'll follow you soon,' he said. 'There is money to be made in Delhi, cutting hair. Girls are keeping it short these days.'

'But men are growing it long.'

'True. So I shall open a barber shop for ladies and a beauty salon for men! Ramu can attend to the ladies.'

Ramu winked at me in the mirror. He was still at the stage of teasing girls on their way to school or college.

The snip of Deep Chand's scissors made me sleepy, as I sat in his chair. His fingers beat a rhythmic tattoo on my scalp. It was my last haircut in Pipalnagar, and Deep Chand did not charge me for it. I promised to write as soon as I had settled down in Delhi.

The next day when Suraj was stronger, I said, 'Come, let us go for a walk and visit our crooked tree. Where is your flute, Suraj?'

'I don't know. Let us look for it.'

We searched the room and our belongings for the flute but could not find it.

'It must have been left on the roadside,' said Suraj. 'Never mind. I will make another.'

I could picture the flute lying in the dust on the roadside and somehow this made me sad. But Suraj was full of high spirits as we walked across the railway lines and through the fields.

'The rains are over,' he said, kicking off his chappals and

lying down on the grass. 'You can smell the autumn in the air. Somehow, it makes me feel light-hearted. Yesterday I was sad, and tomorrow I might be sad again, but today I know that I am happy. I want to live on and on. One lifetime cannot satisfy my heart.'

'A day in a lifetime,' I said. 'I'll remember this day—the way the sun touches us, the way the grass bends, the smell of this leaf as I crush it...'

XVIII

Every morning at six the first bus arrives, and the passengers alight, looking sleepy and dishevelled and rather discouraged by their first sight of Pipalnagar. When they have gone their various ways, the bus is driven into the shed. Cows congregate at the dustbin and the pavement dwellers come to life, stretching their tired limbs on the hard stone steps. I carry the bucket up the steps to my room, and bathe for the last time on the open balcony. In the villages, the buffaloes are wallowing in green ponds while naked urchins sit astride them, scrubbing their backs, and a crow or water bird perches on their glistening necks. The parrots are busy in the crooked tree, and a slim green snake basks in the sun on our island near the brick kiln. In the hills, the mists have lifted and the distant mountains are fringed with snow.

It is autumn, and the rains are over. The earth meets the sky in one broad, bold sweep.

A land of thrusting hills. Terraced hills, wood-covered and windswept. Mountains where the gods speak gently to the lonely. Hills of green grass and grey rock, misty at dawn, hazy at noon, molten at sunset, where fierce, fresh torrents rush to the valleys below. A quiet land of fields and ponds, shaded by ancient trees and ringed with palms, where sacred rivers are touched by temples, where temples are touched by southern seas.

This is the land I should write about. Pipalnagar should be forgotten. I should turn aside from it to sing instead of the splendours of exotic places.

But only yesterdays are truly splendid... And there are other singers, sweeter than I, to sing of tomorrow. I can only write of today, of Pipalnagar, where I have lived and loved.

PARTY TIME IN MUSSOORIE

It is very kind of people to invite me to their parties, especially as I do not throw parties myself, or invite anyone anywhere. At more than one party I have been known to throw things at people. In spite of this—or maybe because of it—I get invited to these affairs.

I can imagine a prospective hostess saying, 'Shall we invite Ruskin?'

'Would it be safe?' says her husband doubtfully. 'He has been known to throw plates at people.'

'Oh, then we *must* have him!' she shouts in glee. 'What fun it will be, watching him throw a plate at —. We'll use the cheaper crockery, of course...'

Here I am tempted to add that living in Mussoorie these forty-odd years has been one long party. But if that were so, I would not be alive today. Rekha's garlic chicken and Nandu's shredded lamb would have done for me long ago. They have certainly done for my teeth. But they are only partly to blame. Hill goats are tough, stringy creatures. I remember Begum Para trying to make us roganjosh one evening. She sat over the *degchi* for three or four hours but even then the mutton wouldn't become tender.

Begum Para, did I say?

Not *the* Begum Para? The saucy heroine of the silver screen?

And why not? This remarkable lady had dropped in from Pakistan to play the part of my grandmother in Shubhadarshini's serial *Ek Tha Rusty*, based on stories of my childhood. Not only was she a wonderful actress, she was also a wonderful person who loved cooking. But she was defeated by the Mussoorie goat, who resisted all her endeavours to turn it into an edible roganjosh.

The Mussoorie goat is good only for getting into your garden and eating up your dahlias. These creatures also strip the hillside of any young vegetation that attempts to come up in the spring or summer. I have watched them decimate a flower garden and cause havoc to a vegetable plot. For this reason alone I do not shed a tear when I see them being marched off to the butcher's premises. I might cry over a slaughtered chicken, but not over a goat.

One of my neighbours on the hillside, Mrs K—, once kept a goat as a pet. She attempted to throw one or two parties, but no one would go to them. The goat was given the freedom of the drawing room and smelt to high heaven. Mrs K— was known to take it to bed with her. She too developed a strong odour. It is not surprising that her husband left the country and took a mistress in Panama. He couldn't get much further, poor man.

Mrs K—'s goat disappeared one day, and that same night a feast was held in Kolti village, behind Landour. People say the mutton was more tender and succulent than than at most feasts—the result, no doubt, of its having shared Mrs K—'s meals and bed for a couple of years.

One of Mrs K—'s neighbours was Mrs Santra, a kind-hearted but rather tiresome widow in her sixties. She was childless but had a fixation that, like the mother of John the Baptist, she would conceive in her sixties and give birth to a new messenger of the Messiah. Every month she would visit the local gynaecologist for advice, and the doctor would be gentle with her and tell her anything was possible and that in the meantime she should sustain herself with nourishing soups and savouries.

Mrs Santra liked giving little tea parties and I went to a couple of them. The sandwiches, samosas, cakes and jam tarts were delicious, and I expressed my appreciation. But then she took to visiting me at odd times, and I found this rather trying, as she would turn up while I was writing or sleeping or otherwise engaged. On one occasion, when I pretended I was not at home, she even followed me into the bathroom (where I had concealed myself) and scolded me for trying to avoid her.

She was a good lady, but I found it impossible to reciprocate her affectionate and even at times ardent overtures, so I had to ask her to desist from visiting me. The next day she sent her servant down with a small present—a little pot with a pansy growing in it!

On that happy note, I leave Mrs Santra and turn to other friends.

Such as Aunty Bhakti, a tremendous consumer of viands and victuals who, after a more than usually heavy meal at my former lodgings, retired to my Indian-style lavatory to relieve herself. Ten minutes passed, then twenty, and still no sign of Aunty! My other luncheon guests, the Maharani Saheba of Jind, writer Bill Aitken and local pehelwan Maurice Alexander, grew increasingly concerned. Was Aunty having a heart attack or was she just badly constipated?

I went to the bathroom door and called out: 'Are you all right, Aunty?'

A silence, and then, in a quavering voice, 'I'm stuck!'

'Can you open the door?' I asked.

'It's open,' she said, 'but I can't move.'

I pushed open the door and peered in. Aunty, a heavily built woman, had lost her balance and subsided backwards on the toilet, in the process jamming her bottom into the cavity!

'Give me a hand, Aunty,' I said, and taking her by the hand (the only time I'd ever been permitted to do so), tried my best to heave her out of her predicament. But she wouldn't budge.

I went back to the drawing room for help. 'Aunty's stuck,'

I said, 'and I can't get her out.' The Maharani went to take a look. After all, they were cousins. She came back looking concerned. 'Bill,' she said, 'get up and help Ruskin extricate Aunty before she has a heart attack!'

Bill Aitken and I bear some resemblance to Laurel and Hardy. I'm Hardy, naturally. We did our best but Aunty Bhakti couldn't be extracted. So we called on the expertise of Maurice, our pehelwan, and forming a human chain or something of a tug of war team, we all pulled and tugged until Aunty Bhakti came out with a loud bang, wrecking my toilet in the process.

I must say she was not the sort to feel embarrassed. Returning to the drawing room, she proceeded to polish off half a brick of ice cream.

◆

Another ice cream fiend is Nandu Jauhar who, at the time of writing, owns the Savoy in Mussoorie. At a marriage party, and in my presence, he polished off thirty-two cups of ice cream, and this after a hefty dinner.

The next morning he was as green as his favorite pistachio ice cream.

When admonished, all he could say was 'They were only small cups, you know.'

Nandu's eating exploits go back to his schooldays when (circa 1950) he held the Doon School record for consuming the largest number of mangoes—a large bucketful, all of five kilos—in one extended sitting.

'Could you do it again?' we asked him the other day.

'Only if they are Alfonsos,' he said. 'And you have to pay for them.'

Fortunately for our pockets, and for Nandu's well-being, Alfonsos are not available in Mussoorie in December.

♦

You must meet Rekha some day. She grows herbs now, and leads the quiet life, but in her heyday she gave some memorable parties, some of them laced with a bit of pot or marijuana. Rekha was a full-blooded American girl who had married into a well-known and highly respected Brahmin family and taken an Indian name. She was highly respected too, because she'd produced triplets at her first attempt at motherhood.

Some of her old hippie friends often turned up at her house. One of them, a French sitar player, wore a red sock on his left foot and a green sock on his right. His shoes were decorated with silver sequins. Another of her friends was an Australian film producer who had yet to produce a film. On one occasion I found the Frenchman and the Australian in Lakshmi's garden, standing in the middle of a deep hole they'd been digging.

I thought they were preparing someone's grave and asked them who it was meant for. They told me they were looking for a short cut to Australia, and carried on digging. As I never saw them again, I presume they came out in the middle of the great Australian desert. Yes, her pot was that potent!

I have never smoked pot, and have never felt any inclination to do so. One can get a great 'high' from so many other things—falling in love, or reading a beautiful poem, or taking in the perfume of a rose, or getting up at dawn to watch the morning sky and then the sunrise, or listening to great music, or just listening to birdsong—it does seen rather pointless having to depend on artificial stimulants for relaxation; but human beings are a funny lot and will often go to great lengths to obtain the sort of things that some would consider rubbish.

I have no intention of adopting a patronizing, moralizing tone. I did, after all, partake of Rekha's bhang pakoras one evening before Diwali, and I discovered a great many stars that I hadn't seen before.

I was in such high spirits that I insisted on being carried home by the two most attractive girls at the party—Abha Saili and Shenaz Kapadia—and they, having also partaken of those magical pakoras, were only too happy to oblige.

They linked arms to form a sort of chariot seat, and I sat upon it (I was much lighter then) and was carried with great dignity and aplomb down Landour's upper Mall, stopping only now and then to remove the odd, disfiguring nameplate from an offending gate.

On our way down, we encountered a lady on her way up. Well, she looked like a lady to me, and I took off my cap and wished her good evening and asked where she was going at one o'clock in the night.

She sailed past us without deigning to reply.

'Snooty old bitch!' I called out. 'Just who is that midnight woman?' I asked Abha.

'It's not a woman,' said Abha. 'It's the circuit judge.'

'The circuit judge is taking a circuitous route home,' I commented. 'And why is he going about in drag?'

'Hush. He's not in drag. He's wearing his wig!'

'Ah well,' I said. 'Even judges must have their secret vices. We must live and let live!'

They got me home in style, and I'm glad I never had to come up before the judge. He'd have given me more than a wigging.

That was a few years ago. Our Diwalis are far more respectable now, and Rekha sends us sweets instead of pakoras. But those were the days, my friend. We thought they'd never end.

In fact, they haven't. It's still party time in Landour and Mussoorie.

ON FOOT WITH FAITH

All my life I've been a walking person. To this day, I have neither owned nor driven a car, bus, tractor, aeroplane, motor-boat, scooter, truck or steam-roller. Forced to make a choice, I would drive a steam-roller, because of its slow but solid progress and unhurried finality.

In my early teens, I did for a brief period ride a bicycle, until I rode into a bullock cart and broke my arm, the accident only serving to underline my unsuitability for wheeled conveyance or any conveyance that is likely to take my feet off the ground. Although dreamy and absent-minded, I have never walked into a bullock cart.

Perhaps there is something to be said for sun signs. Mine being Taurus, I have, like the bull, always stayed close to grass, and have lived my life at my own leisurely pace, only being stirred into furious activity when goaded beyond endurance. I have every sympathy for bulls and none for bull-fighters.

I was born in the Kasauli Military Hospital in 1934, and was baptized in the little Anglican church that still stands in this hill station. My father had done his schooling at the Lawrence Royal Military School, at Sanwar, a few miles away, but he had gone into 'tea' and then teaching, and at the time I was born, he was out of a job.

But my earliest memories are not of Kasauli, for we left when I was two or three months old; they are of Jamnagar, a small state in coastal Kathiawar, where my father took a job as English tutor to several young princes and princesses. This was in the tradition of Forster and Ackerley, but my father did not have literary ambitions, although after his death I was to come across a notebook filled with love poems addressed to my mother, presumably while they were courting.

This was where the walking really began, because Jamnagar was full of palaces and spacious lawns and gardens. And by the time I was three, I was exploring much of this territory on my own, with the result that I encountered my first cobra who, instead of striking me dead as the best fictional cobras are supposed to do, allowed me to pass.

Living as he did so close to the ground, and sensitive to every footfall, that intelligent snake must have known instinctively that I presented no threat, that I was just a small human discovering the use of his legs. Envious of the snake's swift gliding movements, I went indoors and tried crawling about on my belly, but I wasn't much good at it. Legs were better.

Amongst my father's pupils in one of these small states were three beautiful princesses. One of them was about my age, but the other two were older, and they were the ones at whose feet I worshipped. I think I was four or five when I had this crush on two 'older' girls—eight and ten respectively. At first I wasn't sure that they were girls, because they always wore jackets and trousers and kept their hair quite short. But my father told me they were girls, and he never lied to me.

My father's schoolroom and our own living quarters were located in one of the older palaces, situated in the midst of a veritable jungle of a garden. Here I could roam to my heart's content, amongst marigolds and cosmos growing rampant in the long grass. An ayah or a bearer was often sent post-haste after me, to tell me to beware of snakes and scorpions.

One of the books read to me as a child was a work called *Little Henry and His Bearer*, in which little Henry converts his servant to Christianity. I'm afraid something rather different happened to me. My ayah, bless her soul, taught me to eat paan and other forbidden delights from the bazaar, while the bearer taught me to abuse in choice Hindustani—an attribute that has stood me in good stead over the years.

Neither of my parents was overly religious, and religious tracts came my way far less frequently than they do today (*Little Henry* was a gift from a distant aunt). Today everyone seems to feel I have a soul worth saving, whereas when I was a boy, I was left severely alone by both preachers and adults. In fact the only time I felt threatened by religion was a few years later when, visiting the aunt I have mentioned, I happened to fall down her steps and sprain my ankle. She gave me a triumphant look and said, 'See what happens when you don't go to church!'

My father was a good man. He taught me to read and write long before I started going to school, although it's true to say that I first learned to read upside down. This happened because I would sit on a stool in front of the three princesses watching them read and write, and so the view I had of their books was an upside-down one; I still read that way occasionally, especially when a book begins to get boring.

My mother was at least twelve years younger than my father, and liked going out to parties and dances. She was quite happy to leave me in the care of the ayah and bearer and other servants. I had no objection to the arrangement. The servants indulged me, and so did my father, bringing me books, toys, comics, chocolates, and of course stamps, when he returned from visits to Bombay.

Walking along the beach, collecting seashells, I got into the habit of staring hard at the ground, a habit that has stayed with me all my life. Apart from helping my thought processes, it also results in my picking up odd objects—coins, keys, broken bangles, marbles, pens, bits of crockery, pretty stones, ladybirds, feathers, snail-shells, seashells! Occasionally, of course, this habit results in my walking some way past my destination (if I happen to have one). And why not? It simply means discovering a new and different destination, sights and sounds that I might not have experienced had I concluded my walk exactly where it was supposed to end. And I am not looking at the ground all the time. Sensitive like the snake to approaching footfalls, I look up from time to time to examine the faces of passers-by just in case they have something they wish to say to me.

A bird singing in a bush or tree has my immediate attention; so does any unfamiliar flower or plant, particularly if it grows in an unusual place such as a crack in a wall or rooftop, or in a yard full of junk where I once found a rose bush blooming on the roof of an old Ford car.

There are other kinds of walks that I shall come to later but it wasn't until I came to Dehra and my grandmother's house that I really found my feet as a walker.

In 1939, when World War II broke out, my father joined the RAF, and my mother and I went to stay with her mother in Dehradun, while my father found himself in a tent on the outskirts of Delhi.

It took two or three days by train from Jamnagar to Dehradun, but trains were not quite as crowded then as they are today and, provided no one got sick, a long train journey was something of an extended picnic, with halts at quaint little stations, railway meals in abundance brought by waiters in smart uniforms, an ever-changing landscape, bridges over mighty rivers, forest, desert, farmland, everything sun-drenched, the air clear and unpolluted except when dust storms swept across the plains. Bottled drinks were a rarity then, the occasional lemonade or 'Vimto' being the only aerated soft drink, apart from soda water, which was always available for whisky pegs. We made our own orange juice or lime juice, and took it with us.

By journey's end we were wilting and soot-covered, but Dehra's bracing winter climate soon brought us back to life.

Scarlet poinsettia leaves and trailing bougainvillaea adorned the garden walls, while in the compounds grew mangoes, lichis, papayas, guavas, and lemons large and small. It was a popular place for retiring Anglo-Indians, and my maternal grandfather, after retiring from the Railways, had built a neat, compact bungalow on Old Survey Road. There it stands today, unchanged except in ownership. Dehra was a small, quiet, garden town, only parts of which are still recognizable now, forty years after I first saw it.

I remember waking in the train early one morning, and looking out of the window at heavy forest trees of every description but mostly sal and shisharm; here and there a forest glade, or a stream of clear water—quite different from the muddied waters of the streams and rivers we had crossed the previous day. As we passed over a largish river (the Song) we saw a herd of elephants bathing; and leaving the forests of the Siwalik hills, we entered the Doon valley, where fields of rice and flowering mustard stretched away to the foothills.

Outside the station we climbed into a tonga, or pony trap, and rolled creakingly along quiet roads until we reached my grandmother's house. Grandfather had died a couple of years previously and Grandmother lived alone, except for occasional visits from her married daughters and their families, and from her unmarried but wandering son Ken, who was to turn up from time to time, especially when his funds were low. Granny also had a tenant, Miss Kellner, who occupied a portion of the bungalow.

Miss Kellner had been crippled in a carriage accident in Calcutta when she was a girl, and had been confined to a chair all her adult life. She had been left some money by her parents, and was able to afford an ayah and four stout palanquin-bearers, who carried her about when she wanted the chair moved, and took her for outings in a real sedan chair or sometimes a rickshaw—she had both. Her hands were deformed and she could scarcely hold a pen, but she managed to play cards quite dexterously and taught me a number of card games, which I have now forgotten. Miss Kellner was the only person with whom I could play cards: she allowed me to cheat.

Granny employed a full-time gardener, a wizened old character named Dhuki (Sad), and I don't remember that he ever laughed or smiled. I'm not sure what deep tragedy dwelt behind those dark eyes (he never spoke about himself, even when questioned) but he was tolerant of me, and talked to me about the flowers and their characteristics.

There were rows and rows of sweet peas, beds full of phlox and sweet-smelling snapdragons, geraniums on the verandah steps, hollyhocks along the garden wall. Behind the house were the fruit trees, somewhat neglected since my grandfather's death, and it was here that I liked to wander in the afternoons, for the old orchard was dark and private and full of possibilities. I made friends with an old jackfruit tree, in whose trunk was a large hole in which I stored marbles, coins, catapults, and other treasures, much as a crow stores the bright objects it picks up during its peregrinations.

I have never been a great tree-climber, having a tendency to fall off branches, but I liked climbing walls (and still do), and it was not long before I had climbed the wall behind the orchard, to drop into unknown territory and explore the bazaars and by-lanes of Dehra.

THE YEAR OF THE KISSING AND OTHER GOOD TIMES

'Seeds of the potato-berries should be sown in adapted places by explorers of new countries.'

So declared a botanically-minded empire-builder. And among those who took this advice was Captain Young of the Sirmur Rifles, Commandant of the Doon from the end of the Gurkha War in 1815 to the time of the Mutiny (1857).

It has to be said that the good captain was motivated by self-interest. He was an Irishman and fond of potatoes. He liked his Irish stew. So he grew his own potatoes and encouraged the good people of Garhwal to grow them too. In 1823, he received a supply of superior Irish potatoes and was considering where to plant them. The northern hill districts had been in British hands for almost ten years, but as yet no one had thought of resorting to them for rest or relaxation. The hills of central India, covered with jungle, were known to be extremely unhealthy. The Siwaliks near Dehra Dun were malarious. It was supposed that the Himalayan foothills, also forest clad, would be equally unhealthy. But Captain Young was to discover otherwise.

Carrying his beloved Irish potatoes with him, Captain Young set out on foot and soon left the sub-tropical Doon behind him. Above 4,000 feet he came to forests of oak and rhododendron, and above 6,000 feet they found cedars, known in the Himalayas as deodars or devdars—trees of the gods. He found a climate so cool and delightful that not only did he plant potatoes, he built himself a small hunting lodge facing the snows.

Captain Young was to make a number of visits to his little hut on the mountain. No one lived nearby. The villages were situated in the valleys, where water was available. Bears, leopards and wild boar roamed the forests. There were pheasants in the shady ravines and small trout in the little Aglar river. Young and his companions could hunt and fish to their hearts content. In 1826 Young, now a Colonel, built the first large house, 'Mullingar' (I see its remnants from my window every morning), on the way up to what became the convalescent depot and cantonment. Others soon began to follow Young's example, settling as far away as Cloud End and The Abbey. By 1830, the twin hill stations of Landour and Mussoorie had come into being.

Those early pleasure-seeking residents took little or no interest in potato growing, but Young certainly did, and the slope beneath his house became known as Colonel Young's potato field. You won't find potatoes there now, only Professor Saili's dahlias and cucumbers; but potato growing had caught on with the farmers in the surrounding villages, and soon everyone in Garhwal and beyond was growing potatoes.

The potato, practically unknown in India before its introduction in the nineteenth century, was soon to become a popular and vital ingredient of so many Indian dishes. The humble aloo made life much more interesting for chefs, housewives, gourmands and gourmets. The writers of cookery books would have a hard time filling out their pages without the help of the potato.

> *For aloo-mutter and aloo-dhum,*
> *Our heartfelt thanks to Captain Young!*

Shimla became the capital of British India, Nainital the capital of the United Provinces. These towns were soon teeming with officials and empire-builders. But Mussoorie remained non-official, the pleasure capital of the princes, wealthy Indians, European entrepreneurs, and the wives and mistresses of all of them. Mussoorie was smaller than Shimla, all length and not much width, but there was room enough for private lives, for discreet affairs conducted over picnic baskets beneath the whispering deodars.

Ah, those picnics! They seem to be a thing of the past, now that you can drive almost anywhere and find a line of dhabas awaiting you. Few people today bother to prepare those delicate sandwiches or delicious parathas when packets of potato chips and other fast foods are to be found at every bend of the road. Stop at any dhaba in the hills and an instant meal of chow mein will be ready for you. Professor Saili tells me that chow mein is now the national dish of Uttaranchal. I believe him. My own family members demand it whenever we are out for the day.

But to return to Mussoorie's easy-going early days, before the missionaries arrived and made their own rules, imposing their ideas of morality upon the inhabitants.

The station's reputation was well established as far back as October 1884, when the local correspondent of the Calcutta *Statesman* wrote to his paper:

> Last Sunday, a sermon was delivered by the Rev. Mr Hackett, belonging to the Church Mission society; he chose for his text Ezekiel 18th and 2nd verse, the latter clause: 'The fathers have eaten sour grapes and set their children's teeth on edge.' The reverend gentleman discoursed upon the highly immoral tone of society up here, that it far surpassed any other hill station in the scale of morals; that ladies and gentlemen after attending church proceeded to a drinking shop, a restaurant adjoining the library and there indulged

freely in pegs, not one but many; that at a Fancy Bazaar held this season, a lady stood up on a chair and offered her kisses to gentlemen at Rs 5 each. What would they think of such a state of society at Home? But this was not all. 'Married ladies and married gents formed friendships and associations, which tended to no good purpose, and set a bad example.

Adultery under the pines? Mussoorie was well ahead of the times. The poor reverend preached to no purpose. And it was just as well that he was not alive in the year 1933, when a lady stood up at a benefit show and auctioned a single kiss, for which a gentleman paid Rs 300, a substantial amount seventy years ago. (A year's house rent, in fact.) The *Statesman*'s correspondent had nothing to say on this latter occasion; his silence was in itself a comment on the changing times.

A few years ago I received a letter from a reader in England, wanting to know if there were any Maxwells still living in Mussoorie. He was a Maxwell himself, he said, by his father's first marriage. From what he knew of the family history, there ought to have been several Maxwells by the second marriage, and he wanted to get in touch with them.

He was very frank and mentioned that his father had given up a brilliant career in the Indian Civil Service to marry a fourteen-year-old Muslim girl. He had met her in Madras, changed his religion to facilitate the marriage, and then—to avoid 'scandal'—had made his home with her in Mussoorie.

Although there are no longer any Maxwells living in Mussoorie, my former neighbour, Miss Bean, confirmed that Mr Maxwell's children from his second wife had grown up on the hillside, each inheriting a considerable property. The children emigrated, but one granddaughter returned to Mussoorie not so long ago, on a honeymoon with her fourth husband, thus keeping up the family tradition.

Mussoorie was probably at its brightest and gayest in the Thirties. Ballrooms, skating rinks and cinema halls flourished. Beauty saloons sprang up along the Mall. An old advertisement in my possession announces the superiority of Madame Freda in the art of 'permanent waving'. Another old ad recommends Holloway's Ointment as a 'certain remedy for bad legs, bad breasts, and ulcerations of all kinds.'

Darlington's Pain-Curer was another certain remedy for all manner of ailments. It was even recommended by His Highness Raja Pratap Sah of Tehri-Garhwal State, whose domains bordered Mussoorie: 'It affords me much pleasure in informing you that the two bottles of Darlington's Pain-Curer, which I took from you, has given extraordinary relief from the rheumatism I have been suffering since last six months. Therefore I request you to send me two bottles more (large size) as I wish to take this valuable medicine with me on my tour through the Himalaya mountains.'

Neither the ad nor his Highness tells us whether you were supposed to apply the potion or drink the stuff. Perhaps you could do both.

By the time Independence came to India, most of the British and Anglo-Indian residents of our hill stations had sold their homes and left the country. Only a few stayed on—elderly folks like Miss Bean who had spent all their lives here and whose meagre incomes did not allow them to settle abroad.

I wonder what really brought me to Mussoorie in the 1960s. True, I had been here as a child, and my mother's people had lived in Dehra Dun, in the valley below. When I returned to India, still a young man in my twenties (I had spent only four years in England), I lived in Delhi and Dehra Dun for a few years; and then, on an impulse, I found myself revisiting the hill station, calling on the oldest resident, Miss Bean, and being told by her that the upper portion of her cottage, Maplewood, was to let. On another impulse, I rented it.

Always a creature of impulse, my life has been shaped more by a benign providence than by any system of foresight or planning.

Well, that was forty years ago, and Miss Bean has long since gone to her Maker, and here I am in the midst of a large family, living in another cottage and doing my best to keep it from falling down.

Perhaps I really wanted to come back to my beginnings. Because it was in Mussoorie in 1933 (the Year of the Kissing!) that my parents met each other and were married.

I have a photograph of them, on horseback, riding on the Camel's Back Road. He was thirty-six then and had just given up a tea-estate manager's job; she was barely twenty, taking a nurse's training at the Cottage Hospital, just below Gun Hill. A few months later they were living in the heat and dust of Alwar, in Rajasthan, and then Jamnagar in Kathiawar, where my father conducted a small palace school. I was not born in Mussoorie but I am pretty sure I had my conception there!

There is something in the air of the place—especially in October—that is conducive to love and passion and desire. Miss Bean told me that as a girl she'd many suitors, and if she did not marry it was more from procrastination than from being passed over. While on all sides elopements and broken marriages were making hill station life exciting, and providing orphans and illegitimate children for the mission schools, Miss Bean contrived to remain single and childless. She was probably helped by the fact of her father being a retired police officer with a reputation for being a good shot with the pistol and Lee-Enfield rifle.

She taught elocution in one of the many schools that flourished (and still flourish) in Mussoorie. There is a protective atmosphere about a residential school, an atmosphere that, although it protects one from the outside would, often exposes one to the hazards within the system.

The schools were not without their own scandals. Mrs Fennimore, the wife of a headmaster at Oak Grove, got herself entangled in a defamation suit, each hearing of which grew more and more distasteful to her husband. Unable to stand the whole weary and sordid business, Mr Fennimore hit upon a solution. Loading his revolver, he moved to his wife's bedside and shot her through the head. For no accountable reason he put the weapon under her pillow—obviously no one could have mistaken the death for suicide—and then, going to his study, he leaned over his rifle and shot himself.

Ten years later, in the same school, another headmaster's wife was arrested for attempted murder. She had fired at, and wounded a junior mistress. The motive remained obscure and the case was hushed up.

In the St. Fidelis' School, circa 1941, a boy asleep in the dormitory had his throat slit by another boy, it was said at the instigation of one of the teachers. This too was hushed up, but the school closed down a year later.

In recent years, there has been a suicide in one public school, and murders (involving students) in two others; also an accidental death by way of a drug overdose. Tom Brown's school days were pretty dull when compared to the goings on in some of our residential schools.

These affairs usually get hushed up, but there was no hushing up the incidents that took place on the 25 July 1927, at the height of the season and in the heart of the town—a double tragedy that set the station agog with excitement. It all happened in broad daylight and in a full boarding house, Zephyr Hall.

Shortly after noon the boarders were startled into brisk activity when a shot rang out from one of the rooms, followed by screams. Other shots followed in quick succession. Those boarders who happened to be in the lounge or on the verandah dived for the safety of their own rooms and bolted the doors. One unhappy boarder however, ignorant of where the man with the gun might be, decided to take no chances and came round the corner with his hands held well above his head only to run straight into the levelled pistol! Even the man who held it, and who had just shot his wife and daughter, couldn't help laughing.

Mr Owen, the maniac with the gun, after killing his wife and wounding his daughter finally shot himself. His was the first official Christian cremation in Mussoorie, performed apparently in compliance with wishes expressed long before his dramatic end.

A couple of years ago I had a letter from an old Mussoorie resident, Col. Cole, now retired in Pune, who recalled the event:

> Mrs Owen ran Zephyr Hall as a boarding house. It was the last Saturday of the month, and Mrs Owen's son Basil was with me at the 11 a.m.–1 p.m. session at the skating rink and so escaped the tragedy that took place about midday, when Mr Owen shot Mrs Owen and one daughter and then shot himself. I do not know what happened to Basil but he was withdrawn from school and an uncle took him over. This was not the end of the family tragedy. An older sister of Basil's in her early twenties was boating on the river Gumpti at Lucknow with her fiance, when a flash flood took place and the strong current drowned them both.

This was not the end of the story, at least not for me.

A few summers ago, while I was walking along the Mall, I was stopped by a stranger, a small man with pale blue eyes and thinning hair. He must have been over sixty. Accompanying him was a much younger woman, whom he introduced as his wife. He apologized for detaining me, and said: 'You look as though you have been here a long time. Do you know if any of the Gantzers still live here? I believe they look after the cemetery.'

I gave him the necessary directions and then asked him if he was visiting Mussoorie for the first time. He seemed to welcome the inquiry and showed a willingness to talk.

'It's well over fifty years since I was last here,' he said. 'I was just a boy at the time.' And he gestured towards the ruins of Zephyr Hall, now occupied by postmen and their families. 'That was my mother's boarding house. That was where she died...'

'Not—not Mr Owen?' I ventured to ask.

'That's right. So you've heard about it. My father had a sudden brainstorm. He shot and killed Mother. My sister was badly wounded. I was out at the time. Now I have come to revisit her grave. I know she'd have wanted me to come.'

He took my telephone number and promised to look me up before he left Mussoorie. But I did not see him again. After a few days, I began to wonder if I had really met a survivor of this old tragedy, or if he had been just another of the hill station's ghosts. But one day, while I was walking along the cemetery's lowest terrace, I found confirmation that Mrs Owens son had indeed visited his mother's grave. Set into the tombstone was a new stone plaque with the inscription: '*Mother Dear, I am Here.*'

NINA

The big circus tent looms up out of the monsoon mist, standing forlorn in a quagmire of mud and slush. It has rained ceaselessly for two days and nights. The chairs stand about in deep pools of water. One or two of them float around with their legs in the air. There will be no show for the third night running, and tomorrow there will be problems, with the ringhands to be fed and the ground rent to be paid: a hundred odd bills to be settled, and no money at the gate.

Nina, a dark, good-looking girl—part Indian, part Romanian—who has been doing the high-wire act for several years, sits at the window of a shabby hotel room and gazes out at the heavy downpour.

At one time, she tells me, she was with a very small circus, touring the remote areas of the Konkan on India's west coast. The tent was so low that when she stood on her pedestal her head touched the ceiling cloth. She can still hear the hiss of the Petromax lamps. The band was a shrill affair: it made your hair stand on end!

The manager of a big circus happened to be passing through, and he came in and saw Nina's act, and that was the beginning of a life of constant travel.

She remembers her first night with the new circus, and the terrible suspense she went through. Suddenly feeling like a country bumpkin, she looked about her in amazement. There were more than twenty elephants, countless horses, and a menacing array of lions and tigers. She looked at the immense proportions of the tent and wanted to turn and run. The lights were a blinding brilliance—she had never worked in a spotlight before.

As the programme ran through, she stood at the rear curtains waiting for her entrance. She peeped through the curtains and felt sure she would be lost in that wide circus ring. Though her costume was new, she suddenly felt shabby. She had spangled her crimson velvet costume with scarlet sequins so that the whole thing was a red blaze. Her feet were sweating in white kid boots.

She cannot recall how she entered the ring. But she remembers standing on her pedestal and looking over her shoulder to see if the supporting wires were pulled taut. Her attention was caught by the sea of faces behind her. All the artists, the ringhands and the stable boys were there, eager to look over the new act.

Her most critical audience was the group of foreign artists who stood to one side in a tight, curious knot. There were two Italian brothers, a family of Belgians, and a half Russian, half English aerial ballet artist, a tiny woman who did a beautiful act on the single trapeze.

Nina has no recollection of how she got through her act. She did get through it somehow and was almost in tears when she reached the exit gate. She hurried to the seclusion of her dressing-room tent, and there she laid her head upon her arms and sobbed. She did not hear the tent flaps open and was surprised at the sudden appearance of the tiny woman at her side.

'Ah, no!' exclaimed the little trapeze artist, laying a hand on the girl's head. 'Never tears on your first night! It was a lovely act, my child. Why do you cry? You are sensitive and beautiful in the ring.'

Nina sobbed all the more and would not be comforted by the kind woman's words. Yet it was the beginning of a friendship that lasted for several years. The woman's name was Isabella. She took the young girl under her wing with deep maternal care.

She showed Nina how to use ring make-up and what colours I looked best at night. She was nimble-fingered and made costumes and coronets for the girl, and taught her grace in the ring. Once she made a blue-and-silver outfit. The first night Nina wore it, she performed solely for her friend, although the circus tent was crowded and appreciative.

JOYFULLY I WRITE

I am a fortunate person. For over fifty years I have been able to make a living by doing what I enjoy most—writing.

Sometimes I wonder if I have written too much. One gets into the habit of serving up the same ideas over and over again; with a different sauce perhaps, but still the same ideas, themes, memories, characters. Writers are often chided for repeating themselves. Artists and musicians are given more latitude. No one criticized Turner for painting so many sunsets at sea, or Gauguin for giving us all those lovely Tahitian women; or Husain for treating us to so many horses, or Jamini Roy for giving us so many identical stylized figures.

In the world of music, one Puccini opera is very like another, a Chopin nocturne will return to familiar themes, and in the realm of lighter, modern music the same melodies recur with only slight variations. But authors are often taken to task for repeating themselves. They cannot help this, for in their writing they are expressing their personalities. Hemingway's world is very different from Jane Austen's. They are both unique worlds, but they do not change or mutate in the minds of their author-creators. Jane Austen spent all her life in one small place, and portrayed the people she knew. Hemingway roamed the world, but his characters remained much the same, usually extensions of himself.

In the course of a long writing career, it is inevitable that a writer will occasionally repeat himself, or return to themes that have remained with him even as new ideas and formulations enter his mind. The important thing is to keep writing, observing, listening and paying attention to the beauty of words and their arrangement. And like artists and musicians, the more we work on our art, the better it will be.

Writing, for me, is the simplest and greatest pleasure in the world. Putting a mood or an idea into words is an occupation I truly love. I plan my day so that there is time in it for writing a poem, or a paragraph, or an essay, or part of a story or longer work; not just because writing is my profession, but from a feeling of delight.

The world around me—be it the mountains or the busy street below my window—is teeming with subjects, sights, thoughts that I wish to put into words in order to catch the fleeting moment, the passing image, the laughter, the joy, and sometimes the sorrow. Life would be intolerable if I did not have this freedom to write every day. Not that everything I put down is worth preserving. A great many pages of manuscripts have found their way into my waste-paper basket or into the stove that warms the family room on cold winter evenings. I do not always please myself. I cannot always please others because, unlike the hard professionals, the Forsyths and the Sheldons, I am not writing to please everyone, I am really writing to please myself!

My theory of writing is that the conception should be as clear as possible, and that words should flow like a stream of clear water, preferably a mountain stream! You will, of course, encounter boulders, but you will learn to go over them or around them, so that your flow is unimpeded. If your stream gets too sluggish or muddy, it is better to put aside that particular piece of writing. Go to the source, go to the spring, where the water is purest, your thoughts as clear as the mountain air.

I do not write for more than an hour or two in the course of the day. Too long at the desk, and words lose their freshness.

Together with clarity and a good vocabulary, there must come a certain elevation of mood. Sterne must have been bubbling over with high spirits when he wrote *Shandy*. The sombre intensity of *Wuthering Heights* reflects Emily Bronte's passion for life, fully knowing that it was to be brief. Tagore's melancholy comes through in his poetry. Dickens is always passionate; there are no half measures in his work. Conrad's prose takes on the moods of the sea he knew and loved.

A real physical emotion accompanies the process of writing, and great writers are those who can channel this emotion into the creation of their best work.

'Are you a serious writer?' a schoolboy once asked.

'Well, I try to be *serious*,' I said, 'but cheerfulness keeps breaking in!'

Can a cheerful writer be taken seriously? I don't know. But I was certainly serious about making writing the main occupation of my life.

In order to do this, one has to give up many things—a job, security, comfort, domesticity—or rather, the pursuit of these things. Had I married when I was twenty-five, I would not have been able to throw up a good job as easily as I did at the time; I might now be living on a pension! God forbid. I am grateful for continued independence and the necessity to keep writing for my living, and for those who share their lives with me and whose joys and sorrows are mine too. An artist must not lose his hold on life. We do that when we settle for the safety of a comfortable old age.

Normally writers do not talk much, because they are saving their conversation for the readers of their books—those invisible listeners with whom we wish to strike a sympathetic chord. Of course, we talk freely with our friends, but we are reserved with people we do not know very well. If I talk too freely about a story I am going to write, chances are it will never be written. I have talked it to death.

Being alone is vital for any creative writer. I do not mean that you must live the life of a recluse. People who do not know me are frequently under the impression that I live in lonely splendour on a mountain top, whereas in reality, I share a small flat with a family of twelve—and I'm the twelfth man, occasionally bringing out refreshments for the players!

I love my extended family, every single individual in it, but as a writer I must sometimes get a little time to be alone with my own thoughts, reflect a little, talk to myself, laugh about all the blunders I have committed in the past, and ponder over the future. This is contemplation, not meditation. I am not very good at meditation, as it involves remaining in a passive state for some time. I would rather be out walking, observing the natural world, or sitting under a tree contemplating my novel or navel! I suppose the latter is a form of meditation.

When I casually told a journalist that I planned to write a book consisting of my meditations, he reported that I was writing a book on meditation per se, which gave it a different connotation. I shall go along with the simple dictionary meaning of the verb *meditate*—to plan mentally, to exercise the mind in contemplation.

So I was doing it all along!

◆

I am not, by nature, a gregarious person. Although I love people, and have often made friends with complete strangers, I am also a lover of solitude. Naturally, one thinks better when one is alone. But I prefer walking alone to walking with others. That ladybird on the wild rose would escape my attention if I was engaged in a lively conversation with a companion. Not that the ladybird is going to change my life. But by acknowledging its presence, stopping to admire its beauty, I have paid obeisance to the natural scheme of things of which I am only a small part.

It is upon a person's power of holding fast to such undimmed beauty that his or her inner hopefulness depends. As we journey through the world, we must inevitably encounter meanness and selfishness. As we fight for our survival, the higher visions and ideals often fade. It is then that we need ladybirds! Contemplating that tiny creature, or the flower on which it rests, gives one the hope—better, the certainty—that there is more to life than interest rates, dividends, market forces and infinite technology.

As a writer, I have known hope and despair, success and failure; some recognition but also long periods of neglect and critical dismissal. But I have had no regrets. I have enjoyed the writer's life to the full, and one reason for this is that living in India has given me certain freedoms which I would not have enjoyed elsewhere. Friendship when needed. Solitude when desired. Even, at times, love and passion. It has tolerated me for what I am—a bit of a dropout, unconventional, idiosyncratic. I have been left alone to do my own thing. In India, people do not censure you unless you start making a nuisance of yourself. Society has its norms and its orthodoxies, and provided you do not flaunt all the rules, society will allow you to go your own way. I am free to become a naked ascetic and roam the streets with a begging bowl; I am also free to live in a palatial farmhouse if I have the wherewithal. For twenty-five years, I have lived in this small, sunny second-floor room looking out on the mountains, and no one has bothered me, unless you count the neighbour's dog who prevents the postman and courier boys from coming up the steps.

◆

I may write for myself, but as I also write to get published, it must follow that I write for others too. Only a handful of readers might enjoy my writing, but they are my soulmates, my alter egos, and they keep me going through those lean times and discouraging moments.

Even though I depend upon my writing for a livelihood, it is still, for me, the most delightful thing in the world.

I did not set out to make a fortune from writing; I knew I was not that kind of writer. But it was the thing I did best, and I persevered with the exercise of my gift, cultivating the more discriminating editors, publishers and readers, never really expecting huge rewards but accepting whatever came my way. Happiness is a matter of temperament rather than circumstance, and I have always considered myself fortunate in having escaped the tedium of a nine-to-five job or some other form of drudgery.

Of course, there comes a time when almost every author asks himself what his effort and output really amounts to. We expect our work to influence people, to affect a great many readers, when in fact, its impact is infinitesimal. Those who work on a large scale must feel discouraged by the world's indifference. That is why I am happy to give a little innocent pleasure to a handful of readers. This is a reward worth having.

As a writer, I have difficulty in doing justice to momentous events, the wars of nations, the politics of power; I am more at ease with the dew of the morning, the sensuous delights of the day, the silent blessings of the night, the joys and sorrows of children, the strivings of ordinary folk and, of course, the ridiculous situations in which we sometimes find ourselves.

We cannot prevent sorrow and pain and tragedy. And yet when we look around us, we find that the majority of people are actually enjoying life! There are so many lovely things to see, there is so much to do, so much fun to be had, and so many charming and interesting people to meet... How can my pen ever run dry?